TAGG

sman

en ~~THEOLOGIAN~~

Bonnie & Chester O'Brien

BROADMAN PRESS
Nashville, Tennessee

To
Alma Rock Stagg
whose love and devotion made the difference

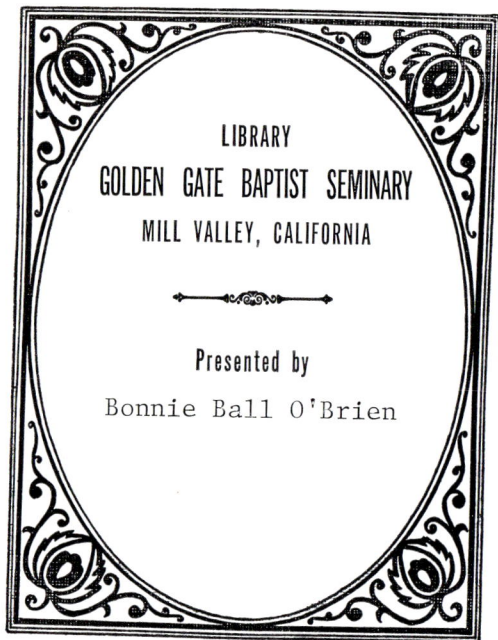

© Copyright 1976 ● Broadman Press
All rights reserved
Item code: 4272-15
ISBN: 0-8054-7215-0
Dewey Decimal Classification: B
Subject heading: STAGG, HARRY P.
Library of Congress catalog card number: 76-18622

Contents

Foreword

It has been my strong conviction for many years that the story of Harry Perkins Stagg needed to be told. He is a man of many facets—but is characterized by a singleness of purpose that is remarkable. Most of the pages of this book after chapter 5 relate in some way to his years as executive secretary of the Baptist Convention of New Mexico, but the chapters are titled so as to remind us of his many talents and experiences.

When he came to New Mexico in 1925, his life hung by a slender thread. But when he was asked to preach for a little church of five members, he was so committed to the Lord that he consented. Thirteen years later he left that pastorate at Gallup to become executive secretary for New Mexico Baptists. Everything he has done since has been in spite of his bad health. In addition to the intrusion of nagging pain and recurring fatigue, major surgery has been scheduled for him fifteen times. Yet even those closest to him in his work remember him as a vital, vivacious, and untiring worker—always wanting to open new doors, dreaming new dreams, and pledging himself to further commitment.

His days as executive secretary—10,950 days—were periods of Baptist expansion in New Mexico. In 1937 Baptist constituents numbered 15,000; thirty years later, there were 90,000. The net worth of the state convention rose from $116,082.00 to $1,460,278.00. And Cooperative Program gifts grew from $14,450.00 to $587,900.00. In connection with this growth, Dr. Stagg salutes the dedicated pastors, missionaries, church leaders, and staff who have worked tirelessly to see this occur.

Many times during his tenure as executive secretary he had

invitations to pastor some prestigious pulpit; three times he was asked to become president of a college. Seven different times he was approached by other states requesting his acceptance of a post with their conventions. This included an invitation from his native Louisiana to become leader of its convention. Although he was grateful for these overtures and made them matters of prayer, he was never released from his call to New Mexico. He says simply, "I knew the place God had for me, and *I was locked into it.*"

Young Harry Stagg was on the first ship to land in France in World War I; years later he became the first executive secretary to pilot a plane owned and operated by the convention he served. He was the first and only New Mexico resident to preach the annual sermon before a Southern Baptist Convention. He was the first graduate from the Baptist Bible Institute (now New Orleans Baptist Theological Seminary) to be named as a member of their Board. He was a member of the first Radio Commission of the Southern Baptist Convention, and his thirty years as executive secretary represent the longest tenure in the Southern Baptist Convention for those in a similar position.

When Harry Stagg came to New Mexico, there were less than one hundred miles of paved roads in the entire state. Today the beautiful Pan-American Highway spans the state from north to south—it reaches toward Alaska and down toward South America—and Interstate 40 takes the traveler comfortably from east to west. Besides these modern roads, there are thousands of miles of wonderful highways which take one all over this enchanting state. But no pavement can ever cover the steps which Harry and Alma Stagg have made in New Mexico.

Because of her commitment to the cause of missions, all author's proceeds from this book will go to carry the message of Christ to mission points in this state. It is my prayer that this book will be a source of inspiration to all who open its pages—that from it we shall all be committed to do more wherever we serve our Lord.

Chester O'Brien, Jr., Executive Director
Baptist Convention of New Mexico

Introduction

He came to New Mexico to die. And he did, symbolically. But out of that death issued *resurrection!* The promise of Jesus is sure: "For whosoever will save his life shall lose it; but whosoever shall lose his life for my sake and the gospel's, the same shall save it" (Mark 8:35)!

Resurrection came about for both Harry P. Stagg and the Baptist Convention of New Mexico. For thirteen years God manifested the resurrection dynamic of the gospel in Gallup, New Mexico, through this man, who much of the time was so ill that he spent the entire week in bed, rising only long enough to preach on Sunday morning. In 1937 he was called to become Executive Secretary-Treasurer of the Baptist Convention of New Mexico.

Circumstances could hardly be more dismal than those which confronted him. Again and again it was through the dynamic quality of this man that a discouraged, defeated convention was "resurrected"—by the challenge of his preaching, by the boldness of his faith, by the daring of his commitment, by the magnitude of his vision. He was God's instrument to lead New Mexico Baptists out of the difficulties of that moment in their history—difficulties that defy description and comprehension in this age of affluence. He urged them to liquidate their indebtedness and to unite their hearts and resources in increasingly great mission undertakings, daring them to believe that with God nothing is impossible.

After thirty-five years of intimate association with Harry Stagg, during which time it has been my wonderful and rare privilege to know Baptists all over the world, I can truthfully say that

7

no one I have ever met more faithfully incorporates the spirit of Jesus Christ. Few have equaled his degree of commitment to Christ as Lord.

One of the major qualities of his life is that implied in the opening paragraph—he willingly lost himself for Christ's sake and the gospel's. He was a grain of wheat who perished and therefore brought forth abundant fruit.

Another characteristic was his oneness with the people. He *cared*, intensely and personally, for individuals and for churches. He knew how to rejoice with those who rejoiced and how to weep with those who sorrowed. His perceptive mind and heart enabled him to readily recognize acute problems. His compassion caused him to minister in love. He was *one* with the Baptists of New Mexico. More than one disgruntled person discovered that the heart of the Baptists of New Mexico belonged to Harry Stagg—that is, to the Lord Jesus Christ first, but to their beloved executive secretary second. They knew that he willingly and joyfully sacrificed himself for the cause of Christ. I have never known him to do one *political* thing. His concern always was the will of God, the body of Christ, the evangelization of the entire world.

His creativity as a preacher was unique. This, of course, was inspired by the Holy Spirit, who empowered him in an extraordinary manner. He had the capacity of taking a news item unnoticed by others and of weaving a great biblical sermon about it. It might be an article about shoes or a visit to the Los Alamos Nuclear Laboratories or about oxen. The Word of God came alive in a most fascinating and attention-capturing manner. Harry Stagg added to everyday subjects the power of the Holy Spirit, and New Mexico Baptists felt that they were listening to one of the most electrifying preachers of this century.

The boldness of his faith and the magnitude of his vision constitute another characteristic that enabled him to be an extraordinary leader for more than thirty years. Many times logic dictated a less adventuresome undertaking or involvement than the one which he chose. His faith in the promises of God and in the trustworthiness of God inspired New Mexico Baptists again and again to attempt the impossible for Christ. One of the most notable achievements, of course, is Glorieta Baptist Conference Center. But there are many others whose stories will unfold in the pages of his biography.

His humility, genuineness, extraordinary discernment, and keen mind are other characteristics and qualities of this unusual leader. His personal commitment to the lordship of Jesus Christ and his willingness to lose his life for Christ's sake and the gospel's are undoubtedly the outstanding qualities. His loyalty to the Word of God, his conviction concerning the mission of Christians and of the church to evangelize the world, and his surety about proper priorities in the kingdom of God are expressions of his extraordinary commitment to Jesus Christ as Lord.

In the pages of this biography you will encounter one of God's great giants; and you will be inspired repeatedly to exclaim, "to God be the glory."

Joseph B. Underwood, Consultant
Evangelism and Church Development
Foreign Mission Board of the SBC

Acknowledgments

History can be written in a variety of ways. One can make a chronological study and distinguish between one particular year or era and another. Or one can dig out facts and events and dwell upon them. But to see a man struggle to achieve when limited by the economic restraints of his day and completely diverted from his goal because of a very personal encounter in a cruel war; to see a man take a position as leader in a state suffering the trauma of the Great Depression and accomplish goal after goal—this is inspiring history.

To the many friends who wrote saying that this story needed to be told, I am most grateful. For those who have encouraged the writing over these months and who have prayed for this endeavor, I am thankful.

Since any such work involves many people, I would like to acknowledge the following secretaries who, under the direction of Mrs. Eleanore Whitehill, typed the manuscript: Mrs. Billie Hale, Mrs. Helen Rigdon, and Mrs. Judy Case. Interviews with Mrs. Eunice Hoyland, Miss Harriet Gatlin, and Dr. E. A. Herron were of special help. The manuscript prepared by Dr. Herron concerning the Glorieta story, plus information provided by Dr. Bob Evans, Rev. Kenneth Chadwick, and the scientific laboratories in Los Alamos and Albuquerque were most important. Informative letters from Mr. Bill Shearin, Miss Eva Inlow, Dr. Joseph Underwood, and Rev. Jeff Rutherford were extremely useful. Historical data from the Baptist Convention of New Mexico plus the usage of private papers from Dr. Stagg's files have been invaluable. In addition, Dr. Stagg himself has been available for taping, conferences, and research. His wife and daughters have been most gracious in providing important data. And to my beloved husband, I am grateful for hours of research and for his constant encouragement.

There are countless multitudes of pastors and missionaries, staff members from the Baptist Convention of New Mexico, and personnel from Baptist churches all over the state who have spent years of dedicated service in order to provide the degree of stability and growth we enjoy today. To these people and the wonderful churches of New Mexico we are forever indebted. Because this fact is true, many books about many people could be written. The book which has been written views Baptist history through the life of one who has been a vital part of this kaleidoscopic expansion for half a century.

Bonnie Ball O'Brien

I. The Child

During the tragic days of the Civil War, it was not at all uncommon to see a Confederate or Union soldier trudging home for a few days of rest and recuperation. Since transportation was extremely difficult, the boys would walk if they had no horse to ride. One can imagine the joyful welcomes they received, the solicitous care which inevitably surrounded them, and the anxiety which followed them as they returned to the battlefield.

A French Acadian soldier, weary from battle, turned his horse into the lane which led to his home. Ironically, he was accompanied by his black slave, who had gone along to help his master in war as he did in peace. No doubt the young family saw the two approaching and met them joyfully. The father-soldier was hustled inside, and his wife went about the mundane task of emptying his knapsack. All that fell out was a piece of molded bread which she quickly threw to the dog. The dog smelled the bread and turned away, refusing to eat his master's food. It was too much! And Ultima Carrentine Stagg, who saw to the running of the farm, the management of the slaves, the care of the children, and endured the separation from her husband for four long years of war, burst into tears at the sight of the pitiful ration in that knapsack. In the years that followed, the telling of that story was always accompanied by her tears.

At last the war was over, and the surviving soldiers returned home. The South was devastated; Louisiana was bankrupt. Nevertheless, Adolphe Stagg returned to his farm on the Bayou Boeuf near Washington to start anew with energy and thrift—two characteristics associated with his ancestors since the fourteenth century.

Settling into homelife once again, Adolphe and Ultima knew that they had to come to grips with the serious matter of their church relationship. Adolphe, whose father was never affiliated with any church and whose mother was a devout, practicing Catholic, held real doubts as to the accuracy of the Catholic faith and practice. He attended Mass as a boy out of respect for his mother, but the Catholic services somehow just never seemed right to him. Ultima, on the other hand, was from a strict Catholic background, but had never really read the Bible for herself. With mutual agreement they set themselves to the task of serious reading and searching of the Scriptures. Adolphe intended to find the truth, and Ultima's main purpose was to find support for her faith.

And so a religious metamorphosis set in as the two plunged into this study that was to have a far-reaching effect in the lives of so many. As they read, they also prayed and meditated and visited several different churches. After many months of this intensive contemplation, they were both converted; and, believing jointly that the Baptist faith and practice came nearer complying with the Bible than any other, they united with the Mount Olivet Baptist Church, Whiteville, St. Landry Parish, Louisiana, in 1870.

In that time and in that place it was almost unheard of for anyone to leave the Catholic Church for another faith. When this did occur, persecution and ostracism followed. The young Staggs were no exception, but they were not deterred from their chosen path. Indeed, Adolphe almost immediately felt the call to preach and began a colorful ministry that was to last for forty years. He was named the first official Baptist missionary to the French in Louisiana and preached fluently in their native tongue, although he used English at home with his children. Part of the time he would pastor a church on a half-time basis, while his other duties would consume the remainder of his time.

Baptists felt that they had one well suited to his task, wedging an opening in French Catholic Louisiana, in Adolphe Stagg, a man of high repute and extensive influence among his own people. However, the minutes of the association for 1873-1874 show that of the $800 salary promised him, he actually received only $169. Nevertheless, he had traveled 1,430 miles by horseback or buggy, baptized eighteen converts, visited fifty-nine families, and preached forty-five times! Quite a part-time job!

In all kinds of weather he went. Motels and hotels were unheard of in Adolphe's territory during the trying days of the Reconstruction; he stayed in the homes of generous people along the way. Later he confided that he knew where he was welcome by the way he was treated by the children in the home!

During these early years of his ministry, he was asked to accept the position of Parish Assessor and agreed to a four-year term. He was possibly in need of supplementing the fractional salary paid him for his growing family, although he was always civic-minded and believed in doing his part in every good endeavor. Even so, he preached always on Sundays and often during the week. This exposure brought him to the attention of concerned citizens of the state who were alarmed over the growing influence of the gambling machine which had controlled Louisiana politics for twenty-five years. Bribes offered to the state, churches, hospitals, and schools in the form of painfully needed revenue were often too tempting. The people felt that the only way to bring this octopus under subjection was to elect a morally upright legislature.

The search for such men resulted in the election of a number of ministers, farmers, teachers, and doctors. While some of these eventually succumbed to bribery offered, a brand-new legislator, Adolphe Stagg, stood firm. One day as the legislators filed into their chambers, each man found a blank check on his desk. All he had to do was to write on the check what it would take to buy his vote! Adolphe, so aware of this sinister monster, turned his check over and wrote deliberately and firmly across the back, "Not for sale at any price." It is to the eternal credit of those who stood morally firm on this issue that the gambling machine was defeated, and it is with deep regret that we note that every minister who sold his vote that day died within the year.

Ultima Stagg was supportive of her husband in all his work, and she did her share in the difficult task of bearing fourteen

15

children and rearing only five to adulthood. She infused hope and inspiration in her husband, even when circumstances seemed most difficult. Not only did she endure the long separation demanded during the war years, the circumstance which so often accompanied the partial payment of salary, but she also found herself the mainstay of the family while Adolphe was away taking care of his missionary obligations. When he persisted in ministering to the sick during the terrible scourge of yellow fever, she would send a servant out to meet him upon his return home. Adolphe would take the clean clothes she had sent, go to the bayou, and wash himself and his contaminated clothing to avoid contagion. Doctors and nurses were hard pressed to care for all the sick, and Adolphe Stagg undoubtedly saved the lives of many during this tragic outbreak.

The fourth son of this couple was named William Lawrence. He was born in 1867 at Whiteville, near Opelousas, Louisiana, before his parents had become Baptists. He recalled riding behind his father on horseback from church one day and his mother's command to change his Sunday clothes. He enjoyed the former, but not the latter! Growing up in the midst of some ostracism, he sometimes wished his father was not a preacher. Some of the schoolchildren called him "preacher" in contempt; some made fun of his beliefs. Said one: "I am so sinful that if I were converted and baptized in the bayou, all the fish downstream would die."

When William was about eleven years old, however, he began to understand more fully what his father's life and purpose were all about. The gospel Adolphe preached was true, and as the Holy Spirit began to speak to young William's heart, there was a ready hearer. After his conversion, William said that he loved his father even more and rejoiced in the fact that he was a minister. But not until he himself became a fellow preacher of the gospel could he realistically interpret the zeal of his father, the not counting the cost of efforts made, and the strict adherence to the verbal inspiration of the Scriptures. Before William had ever thought of preaching, he overheard someone ask Adolphe if he intended to make a preacher out of William. Immediately came the answer, "I am not in that kind of business."

But God is! And William Stagg, undergirded with a rich background of Bible truth, dedicated to the church, and sustained by his parent's example of purity, integrity, and honor, began to prepare himself for the ministry. He earned his B.A. degree in 1891 and then attended the Southern Baptist Theological Seminary in Louisville, Kentucky. After marrying Lizzie Kate Everett of Red Fish, Louisiana, in 1893, he began his active ministry in the general locale of his boyhood. He served scores of churches in Louisiana in thirteen different parishes as well as holding a position on the Executive Board of the Louisiana Baptist Convention. Since he served as clerk of different associations for over thirty years, no doubt one of his greatest thrills came when one of the Baptist associations was named for his father, the Adolphe Stagg Baptist Association.

Into William's home six children were born and were brought up in the same strict tradition their father had known. They did their share of the work and had their turn at good times. Love and deep regard for each other were nourished and followed the children all their lives. Surrounding their family life was the knowledge that God was in control of this universe, that his word was unalterably true, that his promises were irrevocable, and that he had a plan for every life.

While the young family was living in the Avoyelles Parish in a small community named Hamburg, their third son was born. They named their new baby for the husband of Mrs. Stagg's oldest sister. At this time they lived in the nearby town of Red Fish, where this uncle managed the general store and served as notary public and postmaster. With two older brothers giving him attention, little Harry Perkins found his way into the family easily, and some of his earliest memories date back to this town where he was born on October 1, 1898.

One can imagine this small boy standing mesmerized by the sight of the steamboats coming up the river, docking at the levee, and unloading their cargo at his uncle's country store. And then, with whistles tooting their departure, they would disappear down the Bayou des Glaises. One smiles at the mental picture of the same lad, with heart beating in excitement, climbing into his uncle's fancy surrey with the fringed top and two beautiful horses carrying them to the neighboring town five miles away to attend church. Later, from this same store, he was offered his first ride in an automobile! A salesman from New Orleans had come to call on his uncle and had arrived in a Ford car. He noted the obvious interest of the little nephew and offered him a ride down the road "if you don't mind walking back." No ride was ever more joyfully taken. After driving about two miles, the salesman stopped, and Harry jumped out and very willingly walked back along the levee to the store. A car was a wonderful way to travel!

When the family moved to Poland, several miles south of Alexandria, the old country doctor there took quite a liking to Harry, who was too young to go to school and too little to do much work. While the doctor made his medical rounds in his buggy, he would often take the child with him, and the boy would wait in the buggy while the doctor took care of the patient in each house. During these trips the lad imagined himself a doctor, caring for people's ills and making them well. Who knows what effect the ministering care of his preacher-teacher father and the medical attention of this doctor had on his young, impressionable mind? The urgency to serve others which came in later years seemed to be present in embryonic form even then.

In those days it was very common for the pastors of churches to have other work which helped to supplement their meager salaries and maintain their families. As a result, William Stagg often found himself in the schoolroom teaching or administrating. Later he farmed while carrying on pastoral duties. He tried to be near schools so that his children could have every educational advantage possible in that day.

When they moved to Verda, William was the principal of an academy. The family lived on the first floor of a two-story dwelling, and the chapel was upstairs. This chapel served as the meeting place for the local Baptist church.

One night after church, when the Stagg family had gone to bed and all the lights were out, suddenly there came a loud,

Harry P. Stagg, Armistice Day, November 11, 1918. He had just read the sign—posted in French—announcing the conclusion of the war.

urgent knocking at the front door. Mr. Stagg opened the door to a rather upset gentleman whose son was missing from home. "Perhaps," the man explained, "he went to sleep in church and didn't go home with us." Patiently the minister led him up the stairs to the chapel and found the missing child stretched out on a bench sound asleep. But imagine the preacher's astonishment when he discovered his own son, Everett, asleep as well! The family had not even missed him.

The house at Verda stood on blocks, as most of the homes did. The Stagg boys had a little wagon and a goat who pulled them in it in a most unpredictable manner. One day while William, Jr., was riding in the wagon, the goat took a sudden urge to go under the house. The house was high enough off the ground for the goat and the wagon, but not high enough for poor William's head to miss! He sustained quite a blow when he was rammed into the sill of the house.

When the Staggs moved to Woodworth, the father assumed new pastoral duties there as well as the role of teacher in the school. At Christmastime the whole community gathered together for a Christmas tree. Almost seventy years later, Harry P. Stagg can savor the joy of those hours together and can still visualize the candles burning brightly and the beauty of the decorations and gifts. Foremost in his memory is the warmth of the friendly greetings, the expressions of love and concern, and the wonderful spirit of that meaningful holiday season. Even then, he treasured people most of all!

One winter in Woodworth, the weather was so cold that icicles over three feet long formed along the roofs. This was quite a memorable winter for central Louisiana, which usually enjoyed much milder temperatures during the winter and endured hot, sticky summers.

The railroad chute in that little town intrigued young Harry Stagg, and he must have watched carefully as the coal rolled down the high chute through the force of gravity and found its way into the tinder of the steam locomotive. Undoubtedly he must have wondered how the train could run powered by steam and how the coal figured into the total picture.

One of the more poignant memories of their life in Woodworth concerns the oldest son, Everett, who became afflicted with rheumatism. When he became unable to walk, the family transported him in the baby buggy, making it possible for him to go everywhere with them. This was very embarrassing for him, but he endured it because it was necessary.

Most of the growing-up years of Harry Stagg took place in Garland, Louisiana, about fifteen miles north of Opelousas, the parish seat. The family began to grow cotton on their farm and were rather successful until the boll weevil appeared. The larvae of this weevil so infested the cotton crops that great economic damage followed in its wake. The Staggs thus began to grow sugarcane in the place of cotton. This was a very difficult crop to grow because it demanded a great deal of work. Added to this problem was the threat of the September winds. One year the entire crop was blown until it lay flat on the ground. The cost of harvesting such a crop would have exceeded the profit they would have received for it, so the crop was burned. One can imagine the emotional impact such a loss would have on a growing family, but they would not give way to despair.

In the community of Garland there was a Jewish merchant who had a general store. All the farmers bought goods from him, and he would record their purchases in his ledger. When the harvesttime came and the crops were sold, the farmers would pay their entire bill if they possibly could. The farmers teased the merchant about getting his ledgers mixed up and overcharging them. One story which made the rounds concerned a lady who purchased a sidesaddle. The merchant did not put the item down and later could not remember who had bought the saddle. So he just charged it to several of his customers! If they complained when he gave them their bill, he would say, "Oh, that's just an error." Then he would, with a flourish, mark it off. But they accused him of having collected for eighteen sidesaddles!

During these years at Garland, Harry and his brothers and sister worshiped in a one-room church and went to a one-room school. The little town also boasted a post office housed in the general store, a blacksmith shop, and a railroad station where the Southern Pacific trains ran from Alexandria to Lafayette. When the children had time, they loved to go to the depot and watch the trains arrive, pick up the mail, drop the incoming mail, and then leave in a blaze of glory. The tracks ran through the Staggs' farm; and whenever the trains rolled by, whistling their mournful tune, all work had to stop as they watched the train as far as their eyes could see.

When the boys had time off from school and their chores, they loved to ride the horses; and while they became good riders, they also developed into crack marksmen as they hunted small animals. However, the squirrels were not the only target for Harry's .22 rifle. In the hot, humid days of summer he would wander down to the bayous, where moccasin snakes coiled lazily in the sun. As they lay on the big logs floating in the water, the snakes' heads stuck out of their coils and became perfect bull's-eyes for Harry's gun. The number of these reptiles he shot through the head as he was growing up was legion. Not only was he eliminating a dangerous menace, but he was also developing a skill that served him valiantly during his war years and provided food for his family in a day far removed from his boyhood. The toughness of the life on the farm with its many strenuous chores and demands seemed to prepare him for the arduous months on the battlefields of France.

It was on this farm that Harry trained a yoke of oxen. They were used for plowing the fields and cultivating the ground right along with the mule team. Harry also trained them to a wagon; and in the summer, when the crops were all laid by, he would take his oxen and the wagon into the woods and haul heavy oak barrel stave bolts to the railway station. This would bring much-needed cash for the family to purchase necessities not grown on the farm. It was amazing how much help and service this young yoke of oxen was to the work of the farm, and some of the greatest lessons ever learned by their young trainer came about through his observation of those oxen.

In large families where there is a great deal of work to be done, there seems to be a wonderful organization developed to allocate all the tasks evenly and according to the ages and abilities of those involved. Somehow Harry had become the shoeshine boy for the entire clan; and one can imagine him with sixteen shoes lined up in front of him, polish and brushes handy, and harboring the fervent hope that all the shoes would be the same color! Because of his shoe-polishing chores and the fact that he had coal black hair and a dark complexion, someone started calling him "Nig." The nickname stuck, and many of his associates used it freely. The designation eventually evolved to "Shine," and some of the close family members call him by that term to this day.

One day in August when he was eleven years old, "Nig" went with the foreman of their farm to plow a field. The foreman, John Brooks, was a wonderful Negro man who was a tireless worker and a splendid citizen and who made a significant contribution to the Staggs' farm and family. All day long they plowed, and all day long John Brooks talked to young Harry about becoming a Christian. A revival was being conducted in their church, and the exposure to the gospel in such concentrated form found a receptive heart in the lad. When they arrived at the house late in the afternoon, the foreman told Harry's father, "Nig has religion. And he has *good* religion." He made public his profession of faith in Christ in that church in Garland, and his father baptized him in the bayou. It was the same bayou that would furnish water for their family when their wells would go dry, but it attained a significance for an eleven-year-old boy that day which surpassed its normal purpose and which lives in memory in all its beautiful symbolism of a new walk with his Lord.

The youth basked in the warmth of the spirit and fellowship of the members of his church. His Sunday School teacher was an old Confederate veteran who would gather the boys into a corner of the church and teach them from the pulpit. He made a tremendous impression on the life of Harry; and during the long months of war in France, the thoughts of the young soldier would often go back to the hours spent with his Bible teacher as they studied together.

Music schools also occupied a part of their time at church. Musicians would come for about two weeks and teach their eager students. Shape notes were used, and those with ready minds could learn a great deal in the period of time allotted to the training. There were also study courses held in the church which were well attended and profitable in many areas of spiritual need.

One morning William Stagg returned home from a revival thirty miles away. A neighbor pastor who had been helping in the revival brought Mr. Stagg home in his car. Young Harry was amazed! It always required a whole day for his father to reach that church as he usually traveled, by wagon. And here they were before breakfast with the whole day before them for other things! A firm conviction began to form in the son's mind: with so much to be done in every area of life and so little time in which to do it, if one could conserve time, more work could be done. If his father only had a car, he could save hours of difficult travel by wagon and would be more refreshed when he reached his destination as well.

When Harry Stagg was thirteen years of age he had a very deep and abiding impression that he should become a minister. He made his decision to preach and shortly thereafter went with his father to Alexandria to attend a state convention of Louisiana Baptists. As he sat on the benches, his feet did not touch the floor, but he listened intently to each speaker.

One address in particular made an impact on the boy; it seemed to tie in to his earlier dreams of becoming a doctor, yet would fulfill his desire for a spiritual ministry as well. Dr. George W. Leavell, a medical missionary to China, told of his work in that Asian country, and the needs tugged at the lad's heart in a strange manner. How wonderful it would be, he pondered, to prepare himself as a medical missionary and then go to some foreign field to live out his days serving those in need! We sometimes forget that youth respond most quickly to causes that are worth dying for, that bring out the unselfish spirit of giving, that demand their all. Spoon-fed religion which does everything for the young and demands no commitment in return consistently repels them—they seek something which *is* worthy of their complete dedication.

It was with this yearning to prepare himself to serve others that Harry returned to the farm. One can imagine his frustration when he completed grade school and no high school was available to him! Were these commitments to be laid aside? Should he forget further education and content himself to let the years simply pass?

One of God's favorite ways of preparing his chosen men for service has always been a time of silence in a quiet place where hours alone can be spent, the soul can grow, and God himself can mold that vessel according to the use and purpose for which it was created. Harry had several of these years; and, although he worked long hours on the farm, he spent much time in solitary labor.

Farm tools were taken to the blacksmith's shop, where the plow points were sharpened and the cultivators repaired. Corn was carried to the mill about a mile from their home. He would place the large sacks over the backs of the horses, taking care to equalize the load on either side of the animal. He would then mount the horse and ride to the grinding mill, where a certain portion of their corn would be left as payment for the grinding service. He would dig large holes in the fields, line them with corn stalks and straw, and then place sweet potatoes in this prepared place, where they were carefully covered to preserve their use during long winter months. Along with other members of the family, he would take the wagon filled with cotton to Opelousas or Washington for sale. It seemed particularly delightful to leave the farm and travel to the "city," and fruit would be purchased to take home. Fruit was a special treat because they did not grow it on their land.

The sorghum matured in early summer, and sometimes they would make syrup of the sorghum to use until the sugarcane was ready. They were partial to the cane syrup and usually had enough to last through the winter months into the spring. Sugarcane was shipped commercially to the refineries, and they frequently made and sold syrup commercially. Today when

Harry Stagg sees the prices marked on syrup in the grocery stores, he thinks back to the hard labor which went into making such syrup when he was a lad and wishes fervently that they had received a little more financial reward for their work. Almost everything that appeared on the Staggs' dining table had first been brought in from the fields in some form. Mrs. Stagg canned everything she possibly could, and since there was no refrigeration, other foodstuffs were cared for as well as they could be. Dairy products were lowered into the well for cooling, while cellars and smokehouses provided storage for other necessities. Sometimes in the early spring Irish potatoes would be bought for seed; and because the family had been so long without potatoes, the father would carefully cut the eyes of the tubers and reserve them for planting, while the mother would cook the rest. What a treat for growing children! After the potato plants began to grow in the fields the youngsters were always on the alert to sift through the dirt in which the potatoes were growing and find those that were ready for earliest eating.

Constantly before them was the ministry of the father in the family. The "care of the churches" was his main endeavor, and the provisions made on the farm for the sustenance of the family made his ministry possible. If the church he pastored was some distance away, some child might accompany him or he would travel alone; but if he pastored nearby or in the local village or town, the whole family enjoyed worshiping together.

Community life made demands on him as it had on his father, Adolphe; and William was always a willing participant in any cause for good. There were preparations to be made for sermons; there were weddings; and there were funerals. Meetings of the denomination took him away now and then. The good foreman was indispensable in keeping the farm going, but so were the backs of the young Staggs. Their willingness to help make their living from the soil made their contribution to their father's ministry invaluable.

Their nearest neighbors lived about a mile away. One day there came the terrible news that two of the teenage sons from that family had been drowned in the bayou. They were buried in the Baptist cemetery, although they were not of that faith; and Harry mourned over the loss and the terrible waste of those so young. It seemed so unnecessary to him. Little did he realize in those protected years that he would soon be in the presence of massive slaughter of the very young in another country, on another continent, and in a vastly different set of circumstances.

Mrs. Stagg had a brother who lived in Lecompte, Louisiana. He was a medical doctor and knew that his sister's children did not have the advantage of a high school near them. He offered a wonderful opportunity to Harry: if the youth would take care of the uncle's livestock, room and board would be provided for him to go to school! Harry accepted the offer gratefully and arrived at Lecompte in short order. He was eager to get on with his training and visualized its taking years to complete before he could even dream of leaving for the foreign field as a medical missionary. But perhaps this was part of the plan! After all, his uncle was a doctor himself and would be invaluable to Harry every step of the way as advice was needed in his education.

And so it was that the youth left his father's house. The memory of the security he had known there, the warmth and joy and love, and the certain knowledge that his parents had never spared anything in rearing their children would follow him all the days of his life.

It was September, 1916. In Lecompte, Louisiana, a young man was adjusting to a new life as he cared for livestock, started to school, and eased into a new family situation.

His boyhood days were over.

II. The Soldier

In June, 1914, Archduke Francis Ferdinand and his wife Sophie were sent to Sarajevo, Bosnia, to try to calm some tensions between that province and the mother country, Austria-Hungary. A group which tried to pressure the Austro-Hungarian officials into recognizing the Serb's territorial claims was called the "Black Hand." As the Archduke and his wife motored along and crowds cheered them as they waved, a man jumped onto the running board of the slow-moving car and fired three shots. Two struck Ferdinand and one hit Sophie, who was trying in vain to shield her husband. They died almost immediately.

Because of the assassinations and the strong feeling on the part of Austria-Hungary that the tragedy was perpetrated by the Serbians, war was declared on tiny Serbia on July 28, 1914. By October the Central Powers were at war with the Allies as they entered a war that was to cost more than 8,000,000 lives and 337 billion dollars. Untold auxiliary suffering and privation occurred as country after country entered the four-year war.

There were many causes of the war, some reaching back as far as the early 1800's, but the senseless assassination of Archduke Ferdinand seemed to trigger the world into action as war reared its ugly head.

In America there was shocked reaction. President Wilson had no intention of involving the United States in war and stated that we would remain neutral in principle as well as in fact. However, one could not ignore the awesome magnitude of the atrocities to civilians, the numbers of countries becoming involved, the German sinking of passenger ships which sailed unarmed, or the horror of a new weapon—poison gas. Continued submarine attacks by the Germans against American ships made sustained neutrality by the United States impossible; and there was such growing sympathy for the Allies, combined with the anger toward indignities against the American people, that the President requested Congress to declare war against Germany on April 6, 1917.

The United States was in no way prepared for war, but rapid mobilization began to take place. Our country would help its Allies "make the world safe for democracy," and this would be the "war to end all wars." Troopships began to be filled with our "doughboys" as they sailed toward France singing "Over There." The entry of the United States into the war brought a new burst of morale to the weary Allies as fresh troops began to fight the enemy.

None of this was lost on the high school student in LeCompte, Louisiana. As he worked for his uncle and attended school, news of the war was everywhere. When he realized the need for soldiers and recognized that he, himself, was able-bodied, he felt a strange urgency to go. For some reason that he never understood, Harry Stagg felt that the call to help his country was as pressing upon him as his call to preach the gospel. He discussed these confusing thoughts with his uncle, whose reply was, "If you feel so strongly about this, then it seems you must obey your convictions."

The youth was in a quandary. He felt the extreme pressure of time; what he must do required haste. If he volunteered, perhaps his older brother would not have to go and he could help sustain their parents. Harry also reasoned that to go home to bid his loved ones good-bye would only increase their sorrow and that it would be better just to write them of his decision.

Armed with his sense of duty to country and assured by his uncle that the course chosen had no alternative, Harry Stagg offered himself as a soldier in the regular army at the inducting center in Alexandria. He was then sent to New Orleans to Jackson Barracks, filled to overflowing with soldiers. Many of the new enlistees were placed in nearby tents, sleeping on folding cots placed on the bare ground. In this camp a cannon was fired every morning at 6 o'clock for reveille. One morning those in charge of the cannon lowered its elevation just enough to knock down all the tents as reveille was announced. Instead of the young soldiers getting out of bed that morning in an orderly manner, they scrambled from under the tents in all directions in a very decidedly unmilitary fashion. (Of course, the cannon was only filled with powder, but the blast of air released on the novice soldiers' tents was quite convincing just the same. Someone had had fun at their expense!)

A little later, a group of the soldiers was sent down to the Mexican border to join the First Division of the regular army, which was just returning from a tour into Mexico. These seasoned veterans had all kinds of stories to tell about their recent chase of Pancho Villa. And although the new recruits were not needed inside Mexico, they were required to help guard the border. Headquarters were located at Rio Grande City, and a small group of the young men was assigned to Roma to guard the ferry. They were equipped with two machine guns which were placed on the roof of a flat-topped building where the view was unobstructed. Harry took his turn guarding the ferry along with his buddies.

About half the men in the army were seasoned veterans, some with up to thirty years in the service. They were invaluable help in guiding and training the younger men whose experience was almost nil.

One morning as the bugle sounded at Roma, the men recognized it as a call to arms. At 3 A.M. the soldiers began hastily to get themselves together so they could report for the "emergency." Some reported with ammunition and no gun or vice versa, some with shoes not properly laced, and none really dressed and equipped properly. But they all recognized the drill as an important part of their development and training. Another morning, Harry's tent buddy told him to be quiet and remain perfectly still. When the problem became visible, Harry saw that there had been a tarantula as large as a cup underneath his cot, lurking in the sand.

One of the least welcome occurrences to tent dwellers would be a torrential rain. But that is exactly what happened during the short stay at Rio Grande City. Flood waters up to a foot deep played havoc with all that our soldiers were trying to accomplish.

Soon the news came that they were to report to McAllen, Texas, and would shortly be en route to France! They arrived in that Texas border town and began to be loaded into troop trains about noon on a Sunday. The trek across the nation took almost a week, and the soldiers arrived in New York late the following Saturday. The trains were switched onto sidings, and the men were kept on board. During the night, under the cover of darkness, the men were transferred from the trains to the transport ships which lay waiting their cargo. The trip across the United States was, of course, a great secret for obvious reasons. However, when several trains passed through an area at a nondesignated time, there was speculation as to the movement of our troops.

For several days after boarding ship, the soldiers were kept in the hold to prevent detection in any way. Soon, however, they began to slip out into the harbor through the dense fog and anchored out near the Statue of Liberty to wait for the fog to lift so that they could leave. It was June 10, 1917. Harry was eighteen years old.

The transport ships were not luxury liners! They were fruit ships belonging to the United Fruit Company, which shipped fruit from South America to North America. There were five transports in this convoy with two Navy guns fore and aft manned by a Navy crew. A cruiser, the *Seattle,* and about sixteen destroyers surrounded their vessels day and night. The destroyers searched the waters continuously for the omnipresent German submarines and warned of any danger in their pathway. The soldiers were kept on deck through some of the most perilous submarine attack territory, and they used their life preservers as pillars of protection. The German-manned subs seemed determined to prevent any American troops from crossing the Atlantic Ocean.

One morning Harry awoke in the ship's infirmary. He was told that during the night they experienced very rough seas. One of the storm shutters from the porthole above his head had fallen out, striking Harry near the temple. Made of wood and covered with metal, the shutter served as quite a weapon and knocked the young sleeping soldier out, cutting his head as it fell. He carries the scar from that injury to this day.

During the next night or two after this experience, an alarm warned them of an attack by submarines. A sub had come between two of their transport ships. The Americans had felt that the Germans did not know of the presence of the convoy because the sub surfaced as though the ocean belonged to it alone. The captain began to turn the ship hastily with the bow toward the submarine so that the transport would not serve as a broadside target. The guns from either end fired, and the second shot was a direct hit. Two or three destroyers remained close at hand until dawn, patrolling the area, and reported an oil slick. This meant that the submarine had been destroyed, but not before it had done its own damage. It had torpedoed Harry's boat twice, one shot going on either side of the ship as it was turning toward the sub. This caused great excitement among the younger men, although no permanent damage was suffered.

American Expeditionary Forces under General John J. Pershing began landing in France on June 26, 1917. The first transport to land carried Harry Perkins Stagg, American through and through, but with enough French blood coursing through his veins to give this landing special significance. The French people were overjoyed at the offered assistance of the United States and treated the troops gratefully.

After a brief stay on the coast, the soldiers were moved on from St. Nazaire through Paris and toward the front lines between Verdun and Metz. The latter two were French towns, but at the time of the Americans' arrival were strong German forts. There was no time for any semblance of camp life or camp training. The younger men gained their training on a day-to-day

The young pastor—Harry Perkins Stagg—Gallup, NM. Made before 1930.

basis from the older veterans. As they neared the firing line, they were given additional instruction by the choice French Alpine *Chasseurs* and then by the top British instructors. These mentors, of course, had been in the war theater for some time and knew the *modus operandi*. They were put through heavy maneuvers and then through some training under massive gunfire. They would rotate from the front line to the second and then to the third line, coming out of the range of the artillery—but not out of the range of the dirigibles! The young soldiers could also observe the "dog fights" raging over the Western Front as individual pilots fought it out among themselves.

Big sausage balloons were sent up just outside the range of artillery fire for observation purposes. They were invaluable in knowing where certain troops were and how many soldiers could be accounted for. Cables tied to the balloons anchored them to the ground, and the spies on board, peering through telescopes, could see a great deal that was going on below.

Both the Allies and the Central Powers built networks of trenches that stretched for hundreds of miles across France and Belgium. Sometimes less than one hundred yards separated the opposing sides. Between these lines of trenches lay "no man's land." This trench system was the greatest and most complex in history. Second and third lines of trenches would be dug parallel to the front line, while other trenches connected with these in a perpendicular manner so that medicine, food, supplies, and troops could be moved as needed. These trenches served as first-aid stations and protection for the troops. But rain often filled the trenches with water and mud; rats swarmed through the vermin-infested tunnels; and life was miserable. To combat these setbacks, deep dugouts were grubbed out along the trenches where better drainage was installed; thus, the soldiers could "live" in the dugouts with some protection from the elements. When there was a lull in the fighting, battle communiqués reported: "All quiet on the western front."

During the times when the soldiers were not dependent on the dugouts for cover, they were quartered in old barn lofts, with wheat straw serving as their mattresses. Maneuvers in the

34

winter were carried out in painfully cold weather, and the instruction was that boots and shoes should be kept under cover at night so that they would not freeze. Those who forgot or failed to follow the orders found themselves thawing their boots with heat made from little fires fed by wheat straw. Of course, if they were near the front lines, they simply had to suffer the consequences, because no fire could be started since the enemy could easily ascertain their position.

Despite this caution, many of the men lost their feet to the terrible cold of the war; and Harry himself suffered injury as portions of his heels and toes literally sloughed off. In time, however, the healing process restored his feet to near normalcy. Some of the special troops had boots which came up to their hips, and these were very helpful; however, sometimes the mud and slush and half-frozen sludge would be so deep that even the hip boots were not adequate, and the cold liquid would seep into the top of the boot, causing a special kind of agony. For a period of time during this terrible winter, the boys were issued whale oil which they would rub into their feet and limbs to provide a waterproof shield so that the moisture could not soak into their skin and freeze. As Napoleon lost many of his men to the freezing snows on his trek from Moscow to Paris in defeat, so many of our men were casualties of the extreme cold of France that winter.

In one position held by the doughboys, the commanding officers decided that the circumstances were so difficult that it was unwise to try to keep enough men to adequately protect this area. Thus, as secretly as they could, they occupied new trenches behind the mud, hoping that the enemy would think that the original position was maintained. A few soldiers, including Harry, were assigned to stay out there, firing rockets, shooting their guns, and throwing hand grenades occasionally to throw the enemy off guard. The two or three soldiers were in broken-up trenches or shell holes and spaced several hundred yards apart to carry out their ruse. The light of the setting sun gave our soldiers an advantage in that they could see the enemy. But the disadvantage was that the *rising* sun showed our boys in blazing silhouette if they looked over the top of their shelter. In this area there were enemy sharpshooters who were so accurate that if a stick was held up, they could hit it.

In order to locate these snipers, our soldiers contrived a "dummy" soldier, complete with helmet and held aloft with a stick. They would take a position, get a marker, and then let their decoy peer over the top a time or two. Very soon there would be a hit and the direction of the holes in the helmet would be marked. Then they would move down the trench a way and make their lure look over the top again; when it was shot once more, a measure of direction was taken, and the sniper could easily be spotted. Where the lines of fire crossed was, of course, the site of the problem. This spot would be duly marked on our maps, given to the artillery men, and "taken care of."

One morning in the last bit of darkness, Harry himself peered over the top to see if he could detect any trouble spot before the sun came up to reveal his position. Not realizing that the sun was already giving off rays, he saw from a shell hole very near to his position a rifle barrel. It came down to direct aim simultaneously as Harry's head went down! He threw a grenade with all his might into that shell hole. Later on some of the boys investigated the hole. There were footprints all around, as though the sniper had been there all night waiting for his opportunity, at the first break of dawn, to pick off some heads in our line. He almost made it!

Another time while they were maintaining the shell-hole position, they had a premonition that they should change their place, even though they never did stay too long in one spot if they could prevent it. Hardly had they moved to another location before two artillery shells completely blasted out the area where they had just been. On this assignment, Harry was without sleep for five days and nights.

Crawling out into no-man's-land under cover of darkness was a very dangerous operation. This could not be done if there was any hint of moonlight, and absolute silence had to be maintained to prevent betrayal of their position to the enemy. When this could be accomplished, the soldiers went about the difficult task of laying wire entanglements. They used steel coil stakes and would literally screw them into the ground because they could not make noise to hammer them into the ground. Barbed wire—miles of it—would then be stretched from stake to stake across no-man's-land. This was for the purpose of delaying a surprise attack should the enemy suddenly decide to charge over that area. They would get tangled in the wire entrapments and would give our soldiers time for a little preparation.

Sometimes the French would open these entanglements so that they themselves could make attacks on the Germans. They would go out with pliers and cut the wires and lay them back. In the event that electrified wires were set up, rubber-handled pliers, of course, were used. This was a long, tedious process because the wires would have to be tied back together so that the enemy would not see the opening during the day. When sufficient wires had been cut, a surprise trench attack could be made against the German forces.

This process was entirely too slow and laborious for some of our American soldiers. Inventive to the core, they devised a more rapid method which proved to be quite effective. They filled a piece of water pipe with a dangerous explosive called shadite, more destructive than dynamite. They would then slip these pipes under the barbed-wire entrapments; and as soon as the explosion occurred, the trench-raiding party would jump through the opening and be into the enemy trenches before the Germans had sufficient time after the detonation took place to realize what had happened. With this procedure the Americans were able to capture many prisoners who were extremely valuable in giving information as to the location of their troops, their movement, and the whereabouts of artillery.

The matter of spies is a threat to all military engagements, and World War I was no exception. Our soldiers noticed that in many of the small villages most of the town clocks were still there but were not running. In one of the hamlets they noted that the clock periodically showed a different time. Guards were placed to observe the situation, and some spies were soon caught going up at different times during the night to change the time on the clock. They were signaling across the line as to the position of the American artillery. Another spy was caught signaling with a flashlight from the steeple of an old church.

One night it fell the lot of young Harry Stagg to guard two of these spies. They were in the loft of a barn with only one opening and a ladder leading to the loft. Two automatic Colt pistols, strict orders not to move from their positions on the hay, and the youthful soldier served to deter any escape. "That was one night," recalls our veteran, "that I did not get sleepy." The next morning he sighed in deep relief as the MPs came to get his charges.

Another time they came in contact with a spy dressed as an American captain, complete with his aide. The latter was checked out thoroughly and seemed to have his full credentials. When the captain was searched, however, it was noted that he did not have a gas mask, although everything else was in perfect order. Our doughboys knew immediately that he would not risk the danger of being in that area without a gas mask and that he had undoubtedly arranged with the Germans to withhold the use of gas until he had made his investigations on the American side. He was, of course, taken prisoner on the spot.

The use of poison gas was horrible. The Germans first began to use it in 1915, and eventually the Allies used it too. There were several kinds of gas and numerous ways of dispensing it. When the wind was favorable, the gas would be turned loose, and a heavy fog would settle over the enemy lines. The gas masks provided were not too effective, and what benefit they did give did not last long because the container assimilating the poison had to be changed periodically. In hot battles, one did not have too much leisure time for frequent adjustments. If there was an accident or if the mask sustained a bullet hole, there was no recourse.

Sometimes the gas would be mixed with the shrapnel and heavy artillery shells used for demolition. In the attacks made, the artillery would be used to stop oncoming troops. The gas mixed in with the high explosives served very effectively and tragically. Troops not experienced in this deadly combination moved into enemy lines unaware of the double jeopardy which awaited them.

Days between battles were memorable times for Harry. Just before the Battle of Cantigny he secured the permission of a French farmer to use an old barn for worship services. Without a chaplain of his own faith during all these months, Harry eagerly looked forward to the service and vigorously went about the task of cleaning out the barn ahead of time and inviting any who were interested to come and worship with him. He had witnessed during his time in the army to his friends, and they knew of his commitment to the ministry. They trusted him to the extent that some of them, tempted to gamble and/or drink on payday, would give Harry their money to keep lest they, in a weak moment, lose it all. He never kept records of how much each soldier gave him, but he had a pocket for each account, and there was never any question but that each man received all the money he had "deposited."

As the news of the pending service filtered throughout the battalion, Harry waited in great anticipation. When Sunday morning came, the soldiers literally filled that old barn to over-flowing. They sang from memory, without hymnbooks, the songs they had learned in their home churches. And Harry preached to them. It was a wonderful occasion.

That afternoon Harry heard a noise in the loft of the barn as the old rickety ladder was shaken against the ceiling. He looked up and saw a close buddy, Rufus Shelton, from Honey Grove, Texas. The friend said,

"Do you have a minute? I'd like to talk to you."

Harry replied, "Come on."

And while the rest of the boys were out rambling around in the nearby village, Harry Stagg and Rufus Shelton had a very significant talk. Rufus shared the history of his family and his life. He had lost his father when he was a young lad, and Mrs. Shelton had reared a large family made up mostly of boys. He had disappointed his mother with the way he had lived and had eventually become a butch boy on the train. Without asking forgiveness for the grief and sorrow he had caused his mother, without any attempt at assuaging the pain, he had joined the army and had been sent to France. He told Harry that he had thought a great deal about this dilemma and had worried about the sadness he had caused his mother.

"But," he went on, "the service this morning really 'got' me. You have something that I've never had, and I want it."

That morning in the service Harry had mentioned his concern for his own mother, who had suffered through typhoid fever and other ailments. He told how, as a little child, he had thanked the Lord for sparing her life and that now, as a soldier, he feared that her concern over him might be too much for her to endure. And he shared with the boys the fact that he had many times gone back of the old barn where they were worshiping, sat by a hazelnut bush on a little hill, and prayed at dusk that God would take care of his mother.

Rufus was moved by this love and concern which Harry had expressed for his own mother and realized that something very important was missing in his life. On the wheat straw that Sunday afternoon, thousands of miles from home, the love of Jesus was explained to a soldier whose spiritual needs were great. Salvation by grace through faith was made real to Rufus, and he accepted "clear-cut and completely" the way of the cross.

Harry's regiment was selected to make the first all-American attack on the enemy in World War I. Two men from each of the squads were called back of the lines for intensive training for the assault. Harry and another soldier represented their squad and were then used as guides for the actual engagement. The training was just like a play on the stage. A selected area, similar in contour to the land on which the city of Cantigny was built, served as their practice ground. For several weeks the vigorous drills were employed until the chosen men felt that they knew the plan for the siege thoroughly.

The night before the battle, Harry and Rufus Shelton sat at a table in a Red Cross tent together writing letters. There was a mailbox in the tent, and they dropped their letters in it and started to leave. But Harry noted that Rufus had held one of his letters back and that it was placed in his shirt pocket and buttoned safely inside. They left the Red Cross tent together and started back to their quarters to complete preparation for the battle the next morning. As they walked slowly along, Rufus put his arm around the more slightly built Harry and began to tell Harry how much he had meant to him. He was very expressive about the wonderful feeling that he had in being able to write his mother about his changed life and how grateful to God he was for sending the young Christian soldier his way. Then he told Harry that he had a deep-seated feeling that he would not survive this battle—that, indeed, he would not live through the very next day.

"I'm going to be killed in the morning," he ventured. "I won't make it, but it's all right. Everything is all right. But you're going through. The Lord is going to use you in a special way— you will make it. But I will not, and that is all right, for I am entirely ready to go because of my contact with Jesus. Now, you saw me write this letter and place it in my pocket. If possible, tomorrow after I am killed, will you get this letter and send it to my mother? It is my final expression, but I don't want to send it unless I am killed. If I do survive, I will hold it."

And of course, Harry made the sober promise to his friend.

Their orders were to capture the town of Cantigny and straighten out the lines for the new trenches. There was no alternative. When the signal was given at sunrise on May 28, 1918, to "go over the top," they knew they were to capture the objective or die in the attempt. It was a hot battle. The Second Division had been brought up to relieve them, but the Germans broke through at Belleau Wood and Chateau-Thierry. In order to block them, the Second Division was rushed in to plug up that hole in the line, and Harry's division was thus left without support. But the enemy was held back from crossing the Marne River and prevented from making Hindenburg's promised march into Paris. This holding of the Germans enabled Marshal Ferdinand Foch, General-in-Chief of the Allied forces in France, to begin a series of hammering blows against the enemy between Reims and the North Sea which hastened the ultimate end of the war.

And so Harry's regiment made the assigned charge that morning and sustained the loss of fifty-six percent of its men. There were gaps in the line as great as several hundred yards. In Harry's position, the lines led through a wheat field near the edge of the town. On the left wing of the loop they were to straighten while the French troops held anchor. Harry was not far from this hinge position. The enemy had heavy machine-gun emplacements, and they continuously swept that area with artillery fire, cutting the wheat down like a mowing machine as the arc of destruction penetrated the open expanse. Our soldiers proceeded as ordered in two infantry lines with the normal distance between the lines and the soldiers spaced about ten to fifteen feet between each infantry man.

Behind the second infantry line came a row of machine gunners. As new trenches were gained, the machine guns would be set up to protect and hold the new line. The line of fire came to the point where the American rows of troops were lined up to gradually go over that angle. As they passed over it, Harry, in the fourth line, watched his pals go over the top and saw the men being gunned down as the wheat had been and stacked up one upon another. Several hundred yards would be between the men who could get by and proceed toward the desired goal.

By the time it was young Harry's turn to go over the top, the dead were lying four and five deep in some areas. One of the greatest internal battles of his life was fought that day as he struggled with the thought that he could just drop into a shell hole and await the results. Why should he be a sitting duck for the enemy fire? What profit would there be in laying down another life so uselessly? Surely no one could say that he had not already done enough for his country. What atonement could there possibly be just in falling with the rest of the dead, who only moments before were alive as he was and had futures in their dreams, too?

As he wrestled with this temptation, into his courageous heart came the memory of his commitment to his country, his agreement to serve whatever the call, and his orders which called him to victory—or death. So he watched to his right, where for about four hundred yards not a man was standing. When it came his time, he stepped over the top to do whatever was required of him to do that day. He was not cut down immediately and began to inch his way among the dead. He could not believe that he was still alive as he placed one foot before the other, picking his way among his dead comrades. His first thought was "Why?" Why hadn't *he* fallen, too?

In his own words, he recalls the event, still emblazoned on his memory nearly sixty years later:

There came a bright light, brighter than any ordinary sunlight, that came down in a funnel shape, very small, just around my feet and then slanting outward and upward. It seemed that no bullet could penetrate this white light. I was not touched. I walked on ahead and watched to my left, and the men fell as they stepped over for some five hundred yards before another man survived. We made a signal to each other and gradually advanced closer to the other until we arrived at the point of our approved destination, where we had previously planned to establish new lines. We met and fell into a deep shell hole. I knew that there had been a great miracle from heaven.

For a distance of approximately nine hundred yards, Harry Stagg was the only survivor. He was almost in the center of the sweeping artillery fire, yet miraculously was not so much as touched.

The two shell-hole companions knew that counterattacks would come. During the rest of that day they withstood several, but were unable to pass over and beyond their position because of the heavy curtain of artillery and machine-gun fire from their own lines. Sometimes the machine-gun barrels would get so hot from the incessant firing that they would drop in their range, and the bullets would fall into American-held territory. But they stayed with it, and late that afternoon in the fourth counterattack the enemy came very close. Harry's companion received a bullet wound in the head. Spurting blood from the poor youth's wounds covered Harry's gas mask, his chest, and the entire length of his uniform. Harry caught him in his arms, gently laid him back in the side of the shell hole as best he could, and watched alone as the carnage continued.

There was a machine-gun squad up in a nearby tree within firing distance of Harry's shell hole. Harry discovered this new and ominous enemy threat and raised his rifle. His years of shooting the lazy snakes in the bayous of Louisiana stood him in good stead as he took aim at his foes—men made in the image of God but now engaged in the horrors of war. Before he could pull the trigger, however, a large artillery shell hit the tree and scattered the whole operation. The young soldier had further cause for gratitude because he had not had to pull the trigger himself and was grateful to God that in all his months in vicious battle he was never engaged in actual hand-to-hand combat; nor did he ever have to use the cold steel of his bayonet. All the soldiers, upon their arrival in France, had used the old grinding rock with the dripping water and pedals like a bicycle which a French farmer made available to them. They had taken turns, one by one, to run their steel weapons through this sharpening procedure.

Meanwhile, the young doughboy was out in the new no-man's-land because there were not enough American men left alive to form a new trench where it had actually been set. When the American and German lines moved to form their new positions, Harry and those who had survived with him were left about midway between the Allied position and the Germans'. It did not take him long to realize that once more he was in a very precarious position. The knowledge that God had been with him and would continue to be with him sustained him during those ominous hours of waiting.

As dusk came on, Harry knew that somehow he would have to crawl back through the remainder of the wheat without being seen in order to get back to his main line. While he watched, several German patrols came searching for stragglers just like Harry. They would take those they found as prisoners in hope of gaining information which would help them in their plans and operations. He watched several groups; finally one began

44

to come around toward his position. Harry knew that he would have to get out before they got between his shell hole and America's first line trench. Carefully he signaled to his own line so that he would not get shot by his own side as he tried to escape. Of course, the Americans knew that there were a few left out in the new area taken, but they had to be wary of German tricks as well.

When Harry had finally edged and crawled his way back to his own line, a buddy was shocked to see him. One of the other soldiers had reported that he had seen Harry fall as Harry had gone over the top that morning. Immediately the "dead" soldier went to his captain and asked him to rush another telegram to his parents saying that he was alive. But it was several days before the second telegram arrived in Louisiana, relieving the agony and sorrow of the elder Staggs. Miraculously, their son had survived the Battle of Cantigny!

That night as soon as Harry got back into the trenches during the Battle of Cantigny, he asked about Rufus. One of the soldiers reported that he had been killed that day. Harry did everything he could possibly do to find Rufus' body and to carry out his urgent request. But it was impossible due to the sheer volume of bodies lying around the field. As the lines moved forward, these valiant dead were pushed into shell holes and covered until someone could get back to them. As the battle moved forward, other details came and removed as many bodies as they could, each dead soldier still wearing his dog tag.

When they uncovered the body of Rufus Shelton they found, well preserved, the letter to his mother and sent it to her. After the war, when Harry was recovered enough, he went to Honey Grove to see Mrs. Shelton. Rufus' body had been brought back to Texas, and Harry went to the cemetery and visited his grave. It was a very precious occasion, and Mrs. Shelton gave her son's buddy a copy of the letter which had been written only hours before his death. The letter contained a beautiful expression of his readiness to go and the premonition that he would die.

During the night they heard the cries of those who were wounded and had not died. Conscious of the tricks of the enemy, they could not answer every call that came. It was extremely difficult to distinguish between the real pleas for help and the pretended. One feeble cry kept coming during the long dark hours from deep in no-man's-land. The plaintive cry "Help . . . help . . . help" grew weaker and weaker as the night wore on.

By this time some of the French troops had moved over to help the Americans, and the ratio was about half and half. The old experienced veterans warned the youthful soldiers that they should not venture into that area under any circumstances because of the awesome danger. But finally the appeal for help came so pathetically that two men, ignoring any ruse of the enemy to take them prisoners, crawled over the parapet to go out to the supposedly injured man. Those remaining doubled their cover so that relative safety could be had. As the Americans started over, two Frenchmen caught their feet and said, "Wait. If you are determined to go, we will go with you."

So two American soldiers and two French soldiers crawled flat on the ground toward the pitiful sound that was coming through the night. When the circling enemy lights would arc across the field, the four would play dead. After what seemed an eternity, they got back to the trenches with the almost lifeless body of an American soldier and told this story:

Inching their way along they approached the area from which the sounds had come, spreading out so that they could circle and approach the man from different sides while attempting to serve as protection for each other. When they got to the man, they found that he was their first lieutenant, shot to pieces and making what seemed to be his last call for help. They could not carry him because of the enemy threat. Putting their hands beneath his wounded body, they moved him along inches at a time, while enemy flares sent up on parachutes blazed above intermittently, lighting the sky in an unbelievable brilliance. With agonizing delay they were able to inch him along until they got him to safety. It was a moving testimony of bravery, sympathetic understanding, and cooperation in meeting the needs of a desperately wounded soldier.

During the next four days and nights the Americans went

through ten counterattacks and withstood the enemy even without the support of the Second Division. The First Division, depopulated as it was, destroyed seven entire German divisions. The Germans had been so determined to win the first encounter with all-American troops that they had sacrificed seven divisions for the attack. Ludendorff's finest elite troops were thrown in to help overcome the Americans, but to no avail. It was a crushing blow to the enemy. For a time, Harry had in his mementos one of the Ls so proudly worn by one of Ludendorff's fallen men; but later it was lost along with all of Harry's clothing, his Bible, and other small war treasures he had saved.

While they held this line, new wire entanglements had to be set up in no-man's-land. During this long period of time it rained incessantly. The soldiers worked all night with the entanglements and were soaking wet hour upon hour. When they would go back to their trenches before daylight, there was no way to dry their clothing, and the dugout itself would be dank and wet. During this period Harry fell victim to the 1918 influenza which was taking its toll in the United States. The illness was reported to the commander, who came out to see about the youthful soldier. When the youth's forehead was touched to check for fever, his temperature was found to be so high that immediately the commander called a large, strapping soldier and had Harry carried out on his shoulder to a communicating trench at about the third line. Harry was placed in a little Ford ambulance and was driven to a small first-aid station just out of the edge of artillery reach. A number of tents had been pitched, and pads were placed on the ground for the sick and wounded. He was given two aspirins and placed on one of these mats.

Harry declares today that the only thing that saved his life was the comradeship of the other soldiers around him, some of whom were bedfast and others of whom were able to move about. Those who could get up would look after those who could not. There were no doctors or nurses; they were not available. Harry could not get up to go to the mess tent for his meals, and his ambulatory friends brought him juices from canned fruit such as peaches, pears, and apricots. This care and attention from their comrades saved the lives of many American men, including Harry Stagg.

After two weeks, Harry returned to his regular company, still too weak for active duty. The men were ordered to start the march to the other line for the start of the final campaign of the war, what is commonly called the Second Battle of the Marne. This battering offensive began on July 18, 1918, and the Allies never stopped their raging attacks until the Armistice was signed almost four months later.

In his debilitated condition, Harry was hardly able to walk, much less march for miles carrying his gun and ammunition and pack. His companions, sympathetic to his spent physical resources, carried his equipment for him and helped him in every way they could. Even so, he had to march. And he made it!

Preparations for battle were made, and last masses were said. Thinking over his months in the war, Harry realized anew that he had never one time had access to a chaplain of his own faith; indeed, the only ones available to the boys in his division were Catholic priests. And he had no one that night . . . but the memory of other experiences no doubt sustained him as he remembered that God had protected him in a wonderful way, and he prayed that God would guard him in the battles ahead.

During the Second Battle of the Marne, Harry served as infantry guide for the British tanks. The crew in the tanks could not see well enough to ferret out the machine-gun emplacements and artillery positions. The guide was thus necessary as eyes for the tank crew to see where they could not see and to guide and signal so safe passage would be made possible. As they began to make the attack on the German-held city of Soissons, France, Harry tried to do his best in a most difficult situation to protect his crew and yet lead them effectively. Much of the time he did not wear his gas mask because it was such a hindrance to his vision.

The Germans were firing six-inch artillery point-blank at these approaching tanks. Enough poison gas had been mixed in to

Young Harry Stagg standing on the steps of the courthouse, Gallup, NM, where the Baptist congregation met for several years before their building was completed.

stop the British tanks, the Germans hoped, and particularly the infantry guides who made more exact destruction possible. By this time, however, Harry could discern the difference between the smoke coming from the high explosives and the gas. When they approached a gas fog he would throw his mask on quickly to avoid injury.

When they opened their lunches one noon, Harry observed that their corned-beef sandwiches, prepared by our military cooks, were a sick green color. He knew immediately that gas had penetrated their food, and they had nothing to eat that noon.

Sometimes when a gas fog descended on them, they stayed in shell holes or in trenches, where they remained until the mist lifted. This often required several days. Harry was careful enough that he did not suffer the terrible damage that some did. When the mustard gas was used, it would form acid on parts of the body where perspiration would form and burn the soldiers painfully. Even with his caution, however, Harry sustained permanent damage from gas. He breathed in enough that a hole was burned in his nasal passage, where inhaled air always hits.

Although the soldiers were carefully prepared, Harry's physical condition brought about by the flu caused him great concern. His job of guiding tanks was one of the most perilous one could conceive. Usually when one was assigned to this task, he was just written off as dead; no one in that position was expected to survive.

As they approached the city early on that July morning, one of the most spectacular events of the young soldier's military career occurred as he viewed in amazement a regiment of French cavalry in action. They made a furious attack at dawn, but it was over in a flash of time. In mere seconds the enemy was wiped out. British tanks then came and followed through. Even though the crack French cavalry had prepared the way for the tanks, Harry sustained a wound in the left leg from a machine-gun bullet and received a high explosive fragment in his left shoulder and in his right hip. He was incapacitated for further advancement into enemy territory and dropped into a shell hole with another soldier who was grievously wounded.

As best as Harry could, he tried to minister to his buddy's injuries. After the lines moved on far enough, the first-aid rescue teams came as quickly as possible and moved the most seriously injured to safety and care. Harry did not consider his wounds too serious and insisted on waiting. But he felt that his having been wounded saved his life. If he had continued to fight in his weakened condition, his health would have undoubtedly degenerated to the point of death.

He had been without adequate rest and proper food for many months. He had fought in trench warfare where often the food details would be shot down before they could reach the soldiers with supplies. In many areas the water was poisoned with gas, and fresh water had to be brought in.

Once as they were marching across a field, they stumbled onto some cabbages, covered in about two feet of snow. Almost in a state of starvation, they gleefully dug those cabbages out with their bayonets, sliced them, and ate as much raw cabbage as they could. Then they found some old tin cans, melted some snow, and boiled cabbage in those tins. They had neither salt nor pepper for seasoning, but nothing ever tasted better to those hungry troops than the vegetable they gorged themselves with that day. Another time they had gone without sugar for almost a year. When it finally became available, large pans of the sweet stuff were placed out for the hungry soldiers. They were so starved for sugar that they literally scooped it up in their hands and ate it.

For fifteen months Harry had not slept in a bed. He was not only physically exhausted, but was suffering from the horror of seeing so many of his close friends mercilessly slaughtered before his very eyes. His emotions were taut with the tragedy of it all, but he felt that the wounds he sustained at Soissons ultimately saved his life.

With considerable effort the wounded began to make their way back toward the nearest first-aid station. There were many who were grievously wounded. And as they proceeded, Harry heard the woeful groans of a German soldier. Turning to look at him, Harry saw that his whole shoulder had been blown from his body. Taking a first-aid kit from the body of a dead soldier, Harry ministered to the German the best he possibly could. Although they could not talk with each other because of the language barrier, there was a mutual understanding of pain and suffering and horror caused by the terrible mutilation of war. And compassion and understanding passed between the two.

On the trek to the first-aid station many German prisoners accompanied them. One pulled out a beautiful watch to check the time. It was common practice for prisoners to be "relieved" of any treasure which might be useful or wanted by their captors. Since Harry had cherished a lifelong desire for a lovely watch but had seriously doubted that he would ever have one, he decided that he would avail himself of the accepted practice in war that "to the victor belong the spoils." Screwing up his courage to the hilt to claim his trophy, Harry approached the soldier with the watch and indicated through an interpreter that he would like it.

A look of such disappointment and sadness came over the face of the young German that Harry asked the interpreter to find out where the watch had come from. The young soldier told the interpreter that his mother and father had given him that treasure when he had graduated from college and that it meant a great deal to him. Engraved on the watch were meaningful inscriptions from his loved ones. Harry looked at the young man, returned his watch, and through the interpreter told him to keep it well hidden. Harry indicated that when some other American soldier might wish to take it from him as Harry had, the German should by all means tell him the significance of the timepiece; most Americans would be sympathetic with his attachment to it. The German thanked him with a wholehearted expression of gratitude as he pocketed his watch again.

The rescue of the wounded took a great deal of time since only the most seriously wounded were taken back to the medical units first. Others had to either move slowly toward their destination or simply wait their turn. Toward nightfall, a real danger began to grip the attention of Harry and some of his buddies in that so many German prisoners were waiting for their transfer to new quarters. Harry realized that as night came on they would face an emergency in the event that these Germans began to signal for attack. If they had chosen a leader and had had the ambition, they could have rounded up enough guns and ammunition from the fallen to make a significant attack to the rear of our advancing American army and endanger the headway made thus far.

Harry and his comrades spoke to the officers in charge of the first-aid station and some of the wounded officers about the possibility of danger. The military police worked as rapidly as they could to pick these prisoners up and load them in trains, but could not really make a dent in taking care of the immediate problem.

The soldiers who knew the area well remembered that in the valley there were cliffs with big caves which would serve as perfect temporary quarters for these German prisoners of war. Some of the less severely wounded Americans volunteered to guard the caves throughout the night. Consequently, the military police gathered the men up and took them to the caves. Harry was one of six who volunteered to guard them. Each guard lay on a mat because of his wounds but was armed with gun and ammunition. Nine hundred fifty-three German prisoners were housed in the large cave Harry guarded through the night. Turns were taken for guard duty—each man had about two hours guarding and then some time off for sleep. The prisoners were warned by the MPs that if any one of them so much as stepped over a given line at the mouth of the cave, there would be no questions asked; they would be shot immediately.

Throughout the long night, Harry and his five buddies lay on mats in front of the cave, armed with loaded .45 automatic Colt pistols. Of course, if the prisoners had decided to make a sudden plunge through the mouth of the cave, risking the lives of a few to make possible the escape of many, there was actually little that the six wounded American soldiers could have done to deter their flight. The night passed peacefully and without incident. About ten o'clock the next morning the military police came and claimed the prisoners who were to be incarcerated in southern France.

Harry remained in this area, his wounds unattended, through the rest of that day—Friday—and all that night. When he awoke Saturday morning he saw, flying freely and proudly and high in the air, the largest American flag he had ever seen. Attached to the cable of an observation balloon, it seemed to have no earthly attachment whatever.

That afternoon a small ambulance took him to a French hospital train. It arrived about dawn in Paris; and since all the hospitals were filled to overflowing with the wounded, Harry was taken to a large hotel which had been temporarily converted to a hospital. The sheer volume of wounded men, lined up on either side of the halls on stretchers, was so great that the staff had tremendous difficulty in discerning the most severe cases and the extent of each wound and in ascertaining priority among the men. Added to this confusion was the fact that the entire medical staff was made up of French people, who naturally spoke the French language. With all these impediments, it was amazing how efficiently and courageously the service was carried out to dispel the suffering.

The leg and shoulder wounds gave Harry little trouble and began to heal properly. The infected hip, however, began to be an irritating problem, causing considerable illness and concern. Eventually Harry was transferred by means of an American hospital train to Bordeaux in southern France. He stayed in this American hospital until the obstinate wound began to heal, then went through surgical procedures to correct other injuries which he had not reported before his most recent wounds.

After his eventual release from the hospital he was never sent back into active battle, but served two days a week about forty miles from Bordeaux guarding German prisoners. This was light duty compared to the grueling battles Harry had endured; and the prisoners caused no problem, even though the guards were only armed with .38 revolver pistols (which were not likely to cause extensive damage in one who was hit while trying to escape). During the intervals Harry would recuperate and enjoy the abundant grape harvest of the French countryside. It was during this period of rest and abbreviated duty that Harry reached the highest weight level of his life.

On November 11, 1918, Harry was given the first day off of his entire military career. One of his friends, another guard, and he decided to board a train and ride into Bordeaux for the day. They treated themselves to a haircut and, on coming out of the shop, noticed a messenger posting the first telegram of armistice on a light post near the telegraph office. The two soldiers read in French the first notice in Bordeaux. Soon the entire city burst open with the realization that the war was over and that they were on the victors' side! It was an exciting day, and Harry and his friend went to the hospital and visited some of the doctors, nurses, and patients still languishing in their recovery from wounds.

They arrived back at their post later that night. Soon Harry received orders that, as one of the first to enter combat, he would be among the first to return home! What a wonderful day! Perhaps there is no return in all the world like the return home from war.

Because of delays in transportation, however, Harry was not able to leave until after Christmas Day. But because of the promised renewal of home ties and restoration with those he loved, Christmas was a day of joy; and he knew that within a few days he would be leaving battle-scarred Europe behind and sailing for America.

When Harry's company had left the New York harbor almost nineteen months before, there were two hundred fifty hearty young soldiers. Thirteen different times during Harry's active duty with the company, replacements had been sent in to augment the decimated group. Only five eventually returned home. The toll of war is always great.

In due time, appropriate recognition was made for the valor of Harry Perkins Stagg by the Government of the United States of America. In addition to special citations from President Wilson, General Pershing, and General Somerall, he received the

Silver Star, the First World War Victory Medal with three battle clasps, the Purple Heart, and the French Fourragére with a citation from the French Government. The United Daughters of the Confederacy honored him with the War Cross with Oak Leaf Clusters.

These trophies he has treasured all his life. And he has borne in his body during these subsequent years the trauma of the war, for everything that he was to accomplish was carried out in spite of his inadequate physical strength and bad health.

NOTE: During the writing of this chapter, the ninety-first Psalm penetrated my mind and thoughts. I later discussed this with Harry Stagg, who said, "It was my motto throughout the war. I memorized it, and it sustained me." Because of that, portions of the psalm are quoted here . . . a promise of divine protection:

He that dwelleth in the secret place of the most High shall abide under the shadow of the Almighty. I will say of the Lord, He is my refuge and my fortress: my God; in him will I trust. Surely he shall deliver thee from the snare of the fowler, and from the noisome pestilence. He shall cover thee with His feathers, and under his wings shalt thou trust: his truth shall be thy shield and buckler. Thou shalt not be afraid of the terror by night; nor for the arrow that flieth by day; nor for the pestilence that walketh in darkness; nor for the destruction that wasteth at noonday. A thousand shall fall at thy side, and ten thousand at thy right hand; but it shall not come nigh thee. . . . For he shall give his angels charge over thee, to keep thee in all thy ways.

Psalm 91:1-7,11

III. The Student

Home! In all its glory and splendor or in its humble surroundings, there is no place on earth quite like it. And although the weary young soldier did not return to the same town or house which he had left, he returned to the same wonderful, loving family. This group awaiting him for so many hazardous months meant security and safety and peace. Worn in body, mind, and soul, everything that could possibly be done for Harry was performed with hands and hearts filled with love. Even the neighbors helped in many gracious ways; and the little nearby church, where its members worshiped in a tabernacle with a sawdust floor, also extended a warm ministry to him. Harry could neither work nor go to school for a time, and some of the surgery initially performed in France had to be redone in the Pineville Veteran's Hospital.

His first Easter Sunday back in the United States was spent in this hospital where, for thirty days, he had lain flat on his back. Into his room that day entered the whole membership of the Baptist Young People's Union of the Pineville Church. They had walked the entire distance from their church out into the woods where the hospital was situated, some three or four miles away. They were an inspiration and encouragement to him in an abiding way; indeed, their love and concern was the outstanding memory of his stay in that place.

After his removal from the hospital, he had to have care for his teeth. He went to many dentists, all of whom agreed that he must go through the total extraction of his teeth. After all he had been through for so many months, this seemed an impossible sacrifice to make. At last he discovered a dentist in Alexandria who felt that it might be possible for treatment to be rendered which would not require such drastic measures. This dentist began his skilled work, and it has been so successful that some of it remains intact until this day.

While Harry had been in France, his father had moved the family to Pineville, Louisiana, just across the street from Louisiana College, so that the children might be able to continue their educations. There was an academy in conjunction with the school (it is now out of operation), and Harry began to attend classes there. Little by little he was able to attend enough that he completed his high school education.

Excitement began to mount as Harry thought about entering the Baptist Bible Institute (now New Orleans Baptist Theological Seminary). He discussed with the Veteran's Bureau the possibility of their educational advantages for a young preacher. It was agreed that they would pay his tuition, his books, and certain other expenses for the technical education in his chosen field. At last his dreams of becoming a medical missionary on foreign shores seemed to be within reach, and the thrill of it all was exhilarating and stimulating beyond his wildest imagination.

By the time he reached his twenty-second birthday, he was enrolled in the vocational education for the ministry. At the very heart of this school's curriculum, he knew, was a strong emphasis in missions. Some of the finest faculty members to serve in any school had been gathered to teach at BBI. A former Catholic priest from Paris, France, taught French and French Missions. The teacher of Italian and Italian Missions had in his earlier years been a Catholic priest in Rome, Italy. The city of New Orleans itself offered every opportunity for almost any language, culture, or race; and this Christian school took advantage of every occasion to spread the message of Christ.

The youthful student was thrilled beyond words as he met this dedicated faculty, moved among the committed students, and got the "feel" of campus life. He discovered it to be not only a school of missions but a school of prayer as well. The practical aspect of serving while gaining an education was also an exciting prospect.

Harry was assigned a room in the dormitory and moved in joyfully. His roommate was working and would not be available for their first encounter until that evening. When he arrived at last, Harry was in for a real surprise, because before him stood a full-blooded Italian man who could speak no English whatsoever. The teacher of Italian at the school had been instrumental in bringing him to the United States to study; his family remained in Italy until he could earn enough to pay for their passage to America.

Added to the language barrier was the general appearance of the man who stood there, covered with grease and grime and soot from the heating plant where he worked. Harry couldn't imagine living in one room under these circumstances. But then his heart condemned him as he remembered that he was a volunteer for foreign missions and that here before his very eyes and in his own room was a foreigner. The American then realized fully that his initial response was neither Christian nor missionary; and when, after several minutes during which the Italian had taken a complete and thorough sprucing up, dressed in clothing for dinner, and reappeared, Harry saw that he was a very handsome gentleman, kind and thoughtful in manner and pleasant to the core.

Later, as time passed, the man proved to be a wonderful Christian, considerate in every way possible. He never came into the room after Harry had retired and thoughtlessly turned a light on; if he ever had any kind of fruit, candy, or other treat, he always divided it with his roommate. If Harry was out, half of it would be left on his dresser. Many times through the years the Louisianan thanked God for his friend from Rome, and as time passed that year the friend learned English gradually. Harry learned a few words of Italian, so their communication did improve. Before the close of the school year the Italian was able to bring his family to America and to establish a home in New Orleans. After graduation he served for many years with our Home Mission Board in an effective manner.

Harry was studying French along with his other subjects with the desire and hope that he might serve somewhere in a French-speaking country. The provisions made by the school for Christian service in that area were a source of real pleasure to him. And social functions were not uncommon: During his first winter a group of students went out on an excursion boat, sailing down the Mississippi River to the Gulf of Mexico and back. The trip went on into the night, during which time great revelry and raucous merrymaking took place among the other travelers. The students, looking on, yearned for some opportunity to witness to them.

A group of them went to the ship's captain and asked for permission to hold a religious service. He was quite interested and granted their request. He asked his first mate to call the people to order when the students were ready and told them they could have their meeting wherever they desired. On half of the length of the boat was the site for the orchestra and dancing. Down one companionway, in the center and to the rear of the deck, were gambling tables.

An announcement was made that a Christian service was to be held, and the people on board ship became very quiet and courteous. There was music; there were testimonies and Scripture. The group selected Harry Stagg to preach the sermon. He stood on a gambling table in the midst of more money than he had ever seen before (or since) and preached about personal faith in Christ. Later, when the school received reports of these services, the record showed twenty-eight professions of faith! Included in this number was the state commander of the Knights of Columbus. It was a never-to-be-forgotten occasion.

One day the young student was asked to preach at the nearby veteran's hospital. This he was most happy to do because his close comradeship with the soldiers and his own acquaintance with physical suffering were very real. His congregation was dressed in pajamas and robes as he stood to address them. Just as he began the message, one of the patients entered the room. He recognized Harry's voice and rushed with his limited speed toward the preacher. When he reached Harry, he threw his arms around him with deep emotion, and Harry recognized him as one of the five survivors from their company during the war years. Both young men were deeply moved by their reunion in such a place.

After the eight-month school term, opportunity came for Harry to do field work in the northern half of the state under the supervision and direction of Dr. George H. Crutcher, a member of BBI's faculty. Dr. Crutcher had formerly been Executive Secretary of the Louisiana Baptist Convention and had served his denomination well for many years. Harry's major work consisted of teaching study courses on Sunday School and Baptist Young People's Union work. Each month a report was made by his supervisor to the Veteran's Bureau, which helped to finance Harry's school education. It was a wonderful, productive summer that has been joyfully remembered.

That fall Harry was back on the school campus. Situated on a city block, it was much like a beautiful park. When Sophie Newcombe Women's College moved to a new location, Baptists bought their old campus and began their Bible Institute. The buildings were historic and impressive, and the grounds were completely covered with ancient oak trees where moss hung gracefully downward or clung tenaciously to the branches and trunks of the trees. Many species of birds flitted in and out of this miniature forest and warbled their various songs to each other. Squirrels played, unafraid, and darted hither and thither, playing chase and storing up food against the mild winters. It was indeed a beautiful haven.

The year before Harry had missed numerous classes because of his frail health, and the faculty and students were most sympathetic and helpful. This second year, however, proved to be a different matter. His body's strength had never been completely built back after his numerous surgeries and the long months of battle when he went without adequate food for weeks, when satisfactory rest was unheard of, when exposure to freezing weather and soaking rains was endless, and when the relentless parade of war-torn human flesh marched before him. To this was added his stalwart effort to attend all his classes as well as to participate in practical missions and spend his summer traveling and teaching.

It was too much! His depleted physical resources were further exhausted, and he began to miss classes with more frequency. The professors understood when he had to leave during class, and he would sometimes slip out and rest among the oak trees and watch the birds and squirrels in their antics.

One day, however, his roommate entered their quarters to find Harry stretched out across his bed unconscious. He never remembered entering the room, so he could not know how long he had remained unconscious. The friend immediately notified the infirmary, who contacted the doctor. The doctor and his associate came at once, examined their patient, and determined that he was entirely too ill to be moved from that room. They would use the school nurse and whatever personnel they had to attend him in the desperate hope that they could get him to rally.

This grave situation was brought to the attention of the President of BBI, Dr. DeMent. On campus at that time as his guest was a physician from Lexington, Kentucky, a doctor who had served as a medical foreign missionary. The President asked Dr. Anderson if the latter would examine the ailing student and see if he might be able to do something for him. Dr. Anderson went immediately to the dormitory room and, after a thorough investigation of his patient, asked the roommate if he might move into the room in order to take care of the youth himself. The friend gladly accommodated the doctor, and the matter was taken care of on the spot. The semiretired doctor did not leave Harry's bedside except for a period of time each afternoon when he left the nurse in charge for an hour or two while he availed himself of needed exercise.

At one point Dr. Anderson sent an urgent request to the nurse, asking her to rush hot-water bottles and other warming supplies to the room because he thought his patient was dying. Harry's body was cold, and the chill of death itself gripped him. While she was en route the doctor pulled the marble-cold body of the student close to his own, sharing his own body's heat with Harry's lifeless form and willing him back to life. The nurse soon arrived, and warmth was piled all around him. Their heroic attention

First Baptist Church, Gallup, NM. Stone building built in side of hill.
(Not present building.)

was eventually rewarded as Harry began to revive and his strength gradually returned.

One day as Harry was recuperating he learned that his doctor was a friend of the school's President, that they had been seminary students together, and that Dr. Anderson was from Kentucky. Harry asked him if he might know a nurse in Lexington by the name of Maude Sweeney. The doctor replied that he did indeed know her and wondered how his patient knew of her.

"She cared for me in Bordeaux," was his quiet reply.

At last, after six or eight weeks of this confinement, Harry was able to begin attending his classes once more. No one expected him to live, however; and his professors excused him from the normal rules and regulations of classroom procedure and attendance. When he could be in class, he was. Sometimes he left during a lecture to rest under the oaks or go close to the chapel and listen to some of the students rehearse the messages they planned for the next Sunday. He even visited the girls' dormitory as he wished and was generally "spoiled rotten" by teachers and students alike. No one actually expected him to be around very long, and they wanted to make his last days as pleasant as possible.

In a few weeks he had to report to the doctor of the Veteran's Bureau for a checkup. When the examination was completed, the doctor gave him a written order and told him to telephone for a taxicab and to go immediately to the Naval Hospital across the river. He was not to take the time or strength to go back to the school, but he was to telephone his roommate to bring his shaving kit and any clothing and other equipment which he might need as a patient. A strange sensation came over the weakened student, with a peculiar and inexplicable knowledge that he would never come out of that hospital alive if he entered it that day. Instead of going to the hospital as ordered by the doctor, he took a taxicab to the railroad station, telephoned his roommate, and asked him to bring his baggage to the train and also to notify the school authorities that he was going home.

He then telephoned his father in Pineville and informed him of his plight and of his intention to return home in the early hours of the next morning after an all-night train ride. As soon as the train crew arrived, Harry found the pullman porter, who took him immediately into the train and put the languishing student to bed. It was some time before the train pulled out, and before daylight they reached Alexandria. Mr. Stagg had driven from Pineville, just across the river, and was on hand to help his frail son off the train and into the family car.

On reaching home, their doctor was called, and he appeared in short order with his partner. The two men ministered to Harry all day and sat up with him all through the long, torturous night. For ninety days the young man lay almost inert, unable even to feed himself. His mother cared for him tenderly, taking note of every need and ministering to it. He has often said since that his mother had to "raise me twice."

The summer passed with agonizing slowness and stretched into the fall without much progress being made. In the spring he was able to take a few courses at Louisiana College, and in the fall of 1923 he reentered the seminary at New Orleans. Amazingly enough, he completed his seminary degree, Bachelor of Missionary Training, and had more *A*s than anything else. His body might be responding like a Model *T*, but his mind was Lincoln Continental all the way! He was so grateful to have finally reached this important milestone in his training. He took from New Orleans not only the coveted sheepskin, but also the precious memory of dear friends from among the faculty and student body alike. It was always a special pleasure in the years which lay ahead for him to renew fellowship with them.

When he reached home with his brand-new diploma, there was a special feeling among his family about the accomplishment which had been made under such extreme physical duress. There was a tremendous joy and feeling of success in Harry's own heart as he entered Louisiana College that summer to begin his medical course, still intent on the purpose he had held for so many years. Throughout the summer and into the fall and winter terms it seemed that his health would sustain him, but then it began to slip once more; and he was under the constant care of their family physician, Dr. D. I. Payne, who was also a dedicated deacon in their church.

About the first of March, 1925, Dr. Payne called Harry in for a conference. He said, "Harry, a dead missionary is not worth anything to the kingdom of God. If you go on in these laboratory studies, you are going to die, and it won't take long. Now, you must leave school, give up this dream; forget it and go out and just rest. You cannot hold a job or have any heavy responsibilities of any kind. You must rest and relax and give your full attention to the matter of simply surviving. This is the only way you can rebuild your strength."

Immediately Harry was plunged into the very darkest period of his life. His dreams were shattered; and all that he had fought for, studied for, and sacrificed for seemed totally useless and without meaning. He was so distraught that he failed a course in school for the very first time—and only time—in his life. This served to add to his disappointment and frustration to such an extent that he went to the professor and pled for more time and additional coaching. When he took the examination again, he was able to leave all his grades "in order." He was grateful, at least, for that.

Had the whole world caved in upon him? Frail in body, unable to work, his dreams broken into a thousand pieces, he left school. He had no material resources and a very meager wardrobe of clothing. Two of his brothers were in college, and they worked every spare moment possible earning twenty-five cents an hour. Part of this poor income they gladly shared with their sick brother.

And where was God? Had he turned his back on Harry, ignored the one whom he had called to the ministry? Why this gloom, this waste of purpose, this swamp in the wilderness where all his yearnings had died and had suddenly been buried in the mire, unfulfilled?

His frustration was so great that he could not remember that "man's extremity is God's opportunity" and that God deliberately "hath chosen the weak things of the world to confound the mighty." Little did he realize that God had wonderful plans in store for him and that every experience of his life would be used to a divine purpose. Nothing that had come to him would be wasted as he waited out this period of his life, feeling totally useless and without meaning. It seemed to be an endless whirlpool of gloom; he was caught up in it, and there was no escape.

But one day a shaft of light appeared on this bleak horizon and began to play across that dark wasteland of despair. A picture postcard arrived from a BBI classmate who lived in St. Petersburg, Florida. The message written on it was terse and to the point: "I'm going West to do my best. I'll be by your house next Tuesday, and I want you to go with me."

On the following Tuesday the friend arrived as promised. He was driving a brand-new Ford automobile which had been provided by a wealthy family, whose son accompanied him. The youth was not entirely well, and his parents wanted him to enjoy travel at a leisurely pace. Harry's friend had been employed for this purpose and, in addition to being furnished the new car, had an income and enough resources to pay for their needs. They would set Yellowstone National Park as their goal.

Harry insisted that there was no way that he could go. He was sick; he could not work; he had no money or adequate clothing. In short, it would be the height of folly for him to leave his home for such an extended period on such an unnecessary jaunt.

But the friend was adamant. They would travel at a restful pace suited to Harry's strength; money was no problem since there was an income promised; and besides, the journey just might do Harry some good. He had never been out West, and he would be no worse traveling than he would be languishing at home. To emphasize his purpose, the friend stated that he did not plan to leave Pineville without Harry.

At last he was convinced. The Stagg brothers shared some of their limited wardrobe with him and gave him some of their meager income. Dr. Payne had given his patient a final prescription for medication so that Harry could have it filled for emergencies. (The written prescription was never filled and is a treasured possession of Harry Stagg.) They left in style, driving away in their shiny Ford toward the West.

No one could have possibly known that day that Harry Stagg had been standing at the very intersection of his life. His decision to climb into that car heading West sealed his destiny. Without knowing that he was doing anything more than taking a holiday trip, he, standing at the most important crossroad of his life, made a decision which set in motion the events of his entire future existence. Wanting God's purpose accomplished in his life more than anything else, he had unwittingly locked himself into that plan for the rest of his days.

The car pointed north as they drove upward through Louisiana and into East Texas. Their first stop was at Honey Grove, where they visited Rufus Shelton's large family. They then journeyed to nearby Sherman, where they called on another family who had lost a son during the war. They dropped down to Fort Worth and visited Southwestern Baptist Theological Seminary on Seminary Hill. All of this was new territory to them, and they enjoyed it thoroughly.

As they eased along the roadways, they were always careful to take their time and not to pack too much into any one day. They tried to get adequate rest and to eat properly.

When they arrived in Clovis, New Mexico, they went to bed in the motel; but Harry was terribly ill all night long. The next morning they decided to try to press on toward Albuquerque since Harry was ill most of the time anyway, and he told them that being exceedingly sick wasn't too much different from his normal condition. They started the trek down the dirt road and drove about nine miles when the friend, James I. O'Neill, thought for sure that his patient was dying. James whirled the car around toward the nearest ranch home in sight, drove into their yard, and began to call for help. People began pouring out of that house and rushed to their aid.

It is very difficult for young people in our era today to understand that wonderful hospitality back in 1925. In the state, sparsely populated and with a frontier spirit, there were almost

68

always immediate responses to human need and personal involvements which are rare today toward those who are strangers to us.

The family lifted the ailing man out of the car, gently carried him into their home, and put him to bed, while another from their midst jumped into the old car and rushed into town for a doctor. The doctor who was secured was the very one who took care of the veterans' needs in the Clovis area. The physician began to question the young men as to the food Harry had eaten. At last it was determined that some milk drunk the day before was the culprit. It had been stored in a tin bucket in the cafe where they had eaten breakfast the previous morning. Harry had a severe case of ptomaine poisoning. The doctor asked the ranch family if it was convenient to take care of this very ill stranger. They assured him that it certainly was and that they also had plenty of buttermilk, which the doctor said was to be his total diet for about three days and nights.

The doctor returned periodically to check on Harry, and the three remained at the ranch for about two weeks. Their hosts were people they had never heard of before and who had never heard of them, but they were helpful and gracious to the core. And the doctor who cared for Harry did not present a bill of any kind.

The trio planned to leave on a Monday morning. The ranchers, who were Methodists, urged Harry to try to preach to their little church on Sunday afternoon. The group met in a country school building located near the present-day site of Cannon Air Force Base. And so it was that the very first sermon Harry Stagg was to preach in his adopted state was to a Methodist congregation!

It required two days to drive on to Albuquerque, and they arrived in that city late in March of 1925. They went to the barber shop for haircuts, and immediately the barbers began to express deep concern about Harry's health. Many people came to New Mexico during those days to benefit from the warm climate, in hope of being aided in their desperate fight against tuberculosis. The barbers concluded wrongly that this was Harry's predicament until he explained that his lungs were in excellent condition, but that he did suffer from the debilitating effects of the war.

The three made their way to the First Baptist Church on South Broadway and found an exceedingly gracious welcome. They marveled at the manner in which they were received and made to feel at home. Harry met the sheriff of Bernalillo County and discovered that he was the brother of the Staggs' family physician, Dr. Payne, in Pineville. The Albuquerque Paynes were a very faithful family in the First Baptist Church and welcomed Harry as though he had been a long-lost son.

The young men found an apartment just past the railroad spur between North Second and North Fourth. This was really out in the country. Albuquerque was a small village situated largely on the banks of the historic Rio Grande River. While today there are as many people living in the city as there were in the entire state in 1925, then they found lush orchards growing in the fertile valley, where irrigation was available. Peaches, pears, and apples flourished, and splendid grape vineyards were abundant. No house was visible on either mesa. The university was in the country, and cars would often get bogged down in the sandy streets as they would try to go uphill to the school. The old streetcars ran through Central Avenue, now a thoroughfare twenty miles long with brilliant lights marking its path for the planes which today fill the sky overhead.

It was soon discovered that Rev. C. W. Stumph was the Corresponding Secretary of the New Mexico Baptist Convention, and he invited Harry to his office for a visit. They found common ground as Rev. Stumph revealed that he was from Bunkie, Louisiana, very near to Harry's hometown. The older preacher had come to Clovis to serve and then on to Albuquerque to the state office. He knew Harry's grandfather, father, and background in Louisiana; he consequently became intensely interested in the young man and in his physical condition.

When it came time for the Southern Baptist Convention to meet, C. W. Stumph prepared to go. He was on the special committee which formulated and recommended the Cooperative Program for Southern Baptists in 1925. History records that this report was indeed adopted, but before Mr. Stumph left his duties in New Mexico for his responsibilities on the special committee, he called Harry Stagg into his office. He explained that the State Mission Board had approved a missionary for Gallup, the Indian capital of the world. The missionary had gone to Gallup to look over the territory and had reported back that he was not called to be a "foreign missionary."

Brother Stumph then asked Harry whether he felt he would be physically strong enough to go to Gallup and preach to the little mission group until Mr. Stumph returned from the Convention and could take care of the situation on a more permanent basis. He explained that the group met in the county courthouse. When Harry told him he would try to meet that challenge, Mr. Stumph arranged for him to be cared for upon his arrival the next Saturday afternoon.

James O'Neill drove his friend to Gallup in the new Ford. There is no way to describe the condition of the roads in 1925. When one considers the pleasant three-hour drive today over excellent highways, it seems incongruous to realize that one hoped vainly then that the roads would be such that the trip could be made in only a day's time!

A Mr. Malone welcomed them warmly and took them to an apartment provided by one of the mission's charter members. The mission had been organized a few years before as the result of a tent meeting conducted by Rev. A. L. Maddox, who was on the state's evangelism staff. The little group had gone through a difficult period and had secured permission to meet in the courtroom in the old stone county courthouse. In 1923 an earthquake in Gallup had left its mark on the building; a large crack from the roof to the foundation was clearly visible.

On Sunday morning they gathered for Sunday School, two classes meeting in that one room. Mr. Malone taught any adults present, and Gladys O'Sullivan (Kammer), a young girl herself, taught the children. There were about a dozen present that morning, only five of whom were members of the church. Harry preached both services, resting all afternoon in order to be present that night. A telegram came from Rev. Stumph, asking Harry if it was at all possible for him to stay another Sunday. If so, then the corresponding secretary (now called executive director) would come, meet with the five members, and consider the possibility of obtaining a missionary.

It was a wonderfully pleasant and productive week; and when Sunday came and they met once more, the church had the opportunity of approving eleven for baptism! Immediately after the service, the young preacher excused himself, left for his apartment, and dropped into bed exhausted. Brother Stumph then called the group into a business session and reported that there would be a missionary provided them. The church protested that they had the missionary they wanted and that Harry's coming was an answer to their prayers. They pled with their moderator to allow him to stay. A committee was then sent over to Harry's apartment and asked him to return to the meeting, where they explained their desires and hopes and urged him to stay in Gallup under any consideration or limitations placed on him because of his frail health.

This was an entirely new thought to the Louisianan, and he earnestly prayed for guidance. At last he told them that he would stay and try to minister to them as best he could for two months, and at that time they could decide what to do. Those eight or nine weeks, he explained, would give them time to find someone who was well enough to carry on the work required of a pastor. Brother Stumph's explanation of Harry's war injuries and physical limitations did not sway them at all, and it was agreed that the two months would be embarked upon together.

Somehow the two months stretched into thirteen years. And twenty-five years were to pass before Harry Stagg had his first glimpse of Yellowstone National Park.

IV. The Bridegroom

And so the Baptist work in Gallup began to be rekindled under the leadership of the new pastor. Because Harry Stagg had held student pastorates during his days at New Orleans Seminary, his home church in Pineville had called for his ordination to the ministry. He and his brother, William L. Stagg, were ordained the same day in a meaningful service. Thus Harry could begin work with the full credentials needed by a clergyman.

After a few weeks, when it seemed that Harry indeed intended to remain in Gallup, his friend James O'Neill began to accept invitations to preach throughout the state and soon accepted a pastorate himself. He served in New Mexico effectively for many years, moving first to Tularosa as pastor.

Because Gallup was small and the church membership even smaller, Harry soon was able to move among all strata of the population, making friends wherever he went. He preached to his congregation, taught a Sunday School class of young people, visited members as well as prospects, and performed all the ministries a pastor is called upon to do. The congregation was most sympathetic to his physical limitations and allowed him time to rest and recoup his strength as required. With a salary of seventy-five dollars a month he was able to be self-sustaining and to obtain the necessities of life. The problem of walking everywhere he went so used his marginal strength that the purchase of a car seemed necessary, and he consequently negotiated for a Chevrolet automobile.

The first graduating class of Montezuma College, the Baptist school in New Mexico, was scheduled for August of 1925. Alma Rock, petite and vivacious with sparkling black eyes and dark hair, had fulfilled all her requirements for graduation in the spring. She returned to Phoenix, Arizona, to spend the summer with her parents, secure and excited in the knowledge that she had a job—a position!—as teacher of science and math in the Gallup public schools. This seemed to offset the fact that she would be graduated *in absentia,* and she had a happy time getting ready for her new career.

She was to bring to her classroom not only her skill in subject matter but also a vibrancy and timbre of personality that were very appealing. Articulate, friendly, and armed with musical ability, she was an immediate asset to the arena in which she found herself. Her life had always centered in the church and school. Her pattern in Gallup was not to change, and both were enriched by her talents. She was the distilled essence of a remarkable heritage.

The fledgling teacher could trace her maternal lineage back to the seventeenth century to Sir William Vaughan, a distinguished English poet, and to Edward Vaughan, a grantee in the Charter of Virginia in 1609 bestowed by King James. Princes of North Wales appear in her ancestry as well as other noblemen who came to America to help colonize the New World. Colonels, merchants, and a lieutenant governor emerge in the genealogy, as well as a founder of a Baptist church in Newport, Virginia, in 1644. Some of these settled on Virginia land granted to the Vaughan family by King James I of England.

Colonel John Wiley Vaughan built a beautiful and spacious ten-bedroom home in the best possible antebellum style near Independence, Virginia, and found the house quite adequate in which to rear his ten children and entertain his friends. Equipped with a kitchen, storerooms, servants' quarters on the ground level; dining, entertaining, and library rooms on the second; and the bedrooms on the third level, it also boasted a two-level wing plus an attic where the large family stored items they were not using. Alma Rock played in that attic as a very young child midst the copper kettles and out-of-style clothes when her mother, Lillian Dixie, went home to visit her parents.

One day years before this tot was born, Lillian Dixie, home from her finishing school in Lynchburg, Virginia, rode down the streets of Independence on horseback. She passed a young man who was so startled by her beauty that he decided she was the prettiest human being he had ever seen. When they met later, she found that he was a minister, a circuit rider, and a student from Crozier Seminary. She thought to herself, "Here is the man I want to marry—and wherever he asks me to go, I'll go."

In 1902 there was indeed a wedding uniting Lillian Dixie Cox and Clifton Moore Rock in holy matrimony. They set up housekeeping in a quaint log cabin, using a set of handmade maple furniture which had been a gift of the Coxes when they were married.

Clifton Moore Rock was grateful to have a home and a lovely wife. His own mother had died when he was a teenager, and his father, Adolphus Rock, had reared him and his three brothers with the help of various housekeepers. Quite an artisan as a wheelright and cabinetmaker, Adolphus had taught Clifton the skills of the trade. However, the youth felt a strange urgency to preach the gospel and soon left for Norfolk, Virginia, where he lived with a brother and enrolled in the seminary. He worked his way through school by painting for his brother, who was an interior decorator.

After a while, the young Rock family left their picturesque home and returned to the seminary so that Clifton's education could be completed. Mr. Rock also pastored nearby churches; and while he was at Biltmore, a suburb of Asheville, North Carolina, Dr. Millard A. Jenkins highly recommended him as pastor of the Baptist church in faraway Phoenix, Arizona. Even though it was associated with the Northern Baptist Convention, C. M. Rock felt constrained to move West. He moved his family from the only roots they had known and began his ministry in Arizona. After a short pastorate there, he resigned to establish the first Southern Baptist church in the state, Phoenix's First

Southern Baptist Church.

Alma was fourteen years old and undoubtedly marveled at the many differences between the East and West. A good student, she graduated from high school before she was old enough to be permitted to enroll in college and so busied herself with postgraduate courses. The year passed at last, however; and she found herself in Tucson as a student at the University of Arizona. She felt the constraining tug of foreign missions and took courses to prepare for medical skills. However, after about two and a half years in Tucson, she returned home because, along with the large Rock family to provide for and other children to be educated, there was no surplus of funds for her to draw from.

Since Dr. Rock's pastorate was the first Southern Baptist church in Arizona, they had affiliated with the New Mexico Baptist Convention; and he traveled to the adjoining state for conventions and associational meetings. Through this medium the family became acquainted with the Baptist college in New Mexico, and it was arranged that Alma would attend Montezuma College in return for her teaching the children of the faculty. This would provide for her tuition, board, room, and books. She was delighted and continued her premed work.

Since she wanted to take piano lessons and voice as well, she contracted with Dr. Earl Allison, who was head of the music department, to help with his students by keeping records and thus earn piano lessons. She accompanied Mr. J. D. Riddle's voice students in exchange for vocal training. She had received one year of music training as a young child in Virginia and attended another year at the Arizona School of Music in Phoenix while in high school. When she was about twelve years old, she had a bad experience while playing at church; but instead of giving up, she declared that she would certainly do better if given the chance. She more than fulfilled that decision and promise to herself as she worked diligently during her last years of academic training.

Just before she was to graduate, an official from the Gallup school system arrived on the college campus to interview prospective teachers. When he left, he had employed Alma Rock,

Gladys Walker (later Mrs. L. M. Walker, who, along with her preacher-husband, served churches in New Mexico for many years), and Dora Roady (now Mrs. Luther Kitchell). As Alma left for her summer in Arizona, one can imagine the exciting plans laid by the young friends for the coming school year in Gallup.

The new teachers joined Gallup's Baptist Church, where Alma and Gladys Walker became quite a team as pianist and music director. Because they were so faithful in attendance, they became friends with the membership quickly as well as their young pastor. Alma and Harry discovered that they had a great deal in common as the children of Baptist pastors themselves and their earlier desires to be medical missionaries. Due to the financial circumstances of the day and to her realization that she could not support herself and attend medical school at the same time, Alma felt her dream slowly slipping away from her grasp and remembered through her tears, "I found that more important than being willing to go to a foreign field was to be willing to do *whatever* God wanted me to do." But having grown up in a pastor's home, she felt that it would be easier to do anything than to be a pastor's wife!

In November six members from the Gallup church drove to Alamogordo to the state Baptist convention. In one car rode Harry Stagg, the lady who owned the home where he lived, and Alma Rock. Her father would be attending the Convention, and it would be good to see him. The Rock family had been a part of the life of the New Mexico Convention for years, and she was certainly no stranger to it. It would be the first for Gallup's young pastor.

At eleven A.M. sharp on November 11, Armistice Day, the convention paused to observe its memorial service. Only seven years had passed since the war, which was still very much on the minds of Americans. On the spur of the moment, Harry Stagg was asked to participate in this service. He arose and recounted some of his experiences in France in a very moving way. Many in the audience had lost relatives during those terrible days, and some knew of veterans who languished hopelessly in hospitals, yearning for recovery. After the session was over, there were warm and appreciative comments concerning Harry's impromptu remarks, and many marveled at his ability to speak on such short notice.

Christmas came, and Alma returned to Phoenix for the festivities. When New Year's Day arrived, the Rocks had a special guest: Harry Stagg. He was invited by Dr. Rock because Harry could not return to Louisiana for the holidays. The family liked him instantly. He fit into the clan just as he had conformed to his own. It was a happy visit.

Gradually Alma and Harry realized that they were magnetically drawn to each other in an inexplicable way. Alma, remembering her father's good advice that she would do well not to become romantically involved with anyone who had less than robust health, nevertheless began to be convinced that Harry's nature was cut of the cloth which hers required, that his mind complemented and challenged hers, and that his spiritual depth demanded her utmost respect. He was a gentle, gracious spirit; and she came to believe that he could do anything he chose to do, despite his physical limitations.

The young people sat in front of the Western Union building one cold night in the car. As the cold nearly paralyzed them, they discussed their feelings, which seemed much more real than any need for warmth. As Harry poured out his frustrations to the minister's daughter, he wept as he expressed his very real fears that he would not be physically able to do the work he felt called to do, that somehow he would fail, that he had to spend so much valuable time in necessary rest that life was passing him by. He felt that he could not cope with such problems.

She knew that he was at a low ebb and began to bolster him as best she could. She told him that she had come to feel that, sick or well, he could do whatever he set out to accomplish. If God wanted to work through him, the strength would be given

Dr. Harry P. Stagg

as it was needed. With all ninety-five pounds of her being, she believed in the young man sitting in the chill of that evening; and this ardent outpouring of her faith in him warmed them both.

At last, without asking her to marry him, Harry said, "Well, I guess we'd better set a date and get this fixed up!" Alma instinctively understood his proposal and began to try to help him "figure out a date." The Southern Baptist Convention was meeting in Houston in the spring, and Harry wanted to take her along as his bride. She was willing to cooperate, but nevertheless explained that she had signed a contract to teach and that if there was a problem in getting a replacement, she would have to postpone their wedding. She went to the school superintendent and explained their plans to him, but acknowledged her willingness to fulfill her contract. He was gracious and understanding about her request and assured her that they should go ahead with their wedding preparations. He would manage.

About that time, Dr. Rock was returning from Albuquerque, where he had been attending a board meeting. He stopped in Gallup to spend the night and registered at the Harvey House. Harry decided that this would be a good time to ask for Alma's hand in marriage and thus set up an appointment with her father. The train for Phoenix left early the next morning, and the visit had to be the evening before. Harry laid out his plans and hopes before Dr. Rock, but the latter remained silent and noncommittal. Perhaps the younger preacher felt a hesitancy on the part of the older, because Harry said at last, "I think she is going to do what I say—so it is just as well that you answer me now!" Dr. Rock told him that he must think it over and that he would give him an answer the next morning, although it would necessitate his leaving on a later train. The next morning, true to his promise, Dr. Rock went by Harry's apartment and gave him a father's blessing.

The wedding was held at sunrise on April 21, 1926, on the east porch of the family home in Phoenix. Some of the family and guests were seated on the porch while the overflow stood on the lawn for the ceremony. Just as the sun came up over the famed Camelback Mountain, Harry and Alma's vows were said, and a new life for both was begun together.

Immediately after the attendant celebration, the two left in their car, affectionately named "the Sunshine Special." In their possession was enough money for their honeymoon—seventy-five dollars—which had been borrowed for that purpose. As they traveled over the road leading east and south to Houston, they discussed how much it meant to them to have her father perform the ceremony and how nervous her brother Vaughan, the best man, had been. They themselves were filled with a wonderful calm and peace, so sure were they that they were in God's will for their lives.

When they returned to Gallup, they discovered that the church had generously raised their salary to one hundred dollars a month. And with the determination to do their very best reaffirmed, they "settled in" to serve together.

V. The Pastor

Under the capable leadership of the pastor and his wife the church began to grow steadily, albeit slowly. Turnover was a matter to cope with because the population of the town shifted continuously. Their minister was to quip later on that he was able to remain in Gallup because of this very fact . . . the *people* kept moving! Despite his modesty, however, the record shows that the Sunday School averaged an attendance of fifty during 1926; and twenty were baptized into the fellowship of the church whose membership then stood at sixty-seven.

Those who arrived in Gallup with the intent of joining a Baptist church were, of course, directed to the courthouse. This was a surprise to many who had been accustomed to extremely different surroundings when they worshiped. One such inquirer was a new bride from the South, Eunice Loder Hoyland; and as she made her way to the service for the first time, she found a very warm welcome awaiting her. That which moved her to tears, however, was the sound of the pastor's rich southern voice. It was a vestige from home to which she clung. She was near the ages of the Staggs, as well as having a similar geographic background and education. They became lifelong friends.

Even though the total program of the church was carried on in one room of the government building, it "seemed like church" to the members, in spite of the limitations which surrounded them.

One night during the early part of a service, a group of men arrived on the scene for a political rally. The young pastor apprised them of the situation and promised that if they would be seated quietly while the service continued, they would be delayed only thirty minutes. The men agreed to this suggestion. But such experiences, compounded by their steady growth and need for space, made them yearn for a building of their own which would not only be architecturally suitable for church activities but would be available to them at all times.

The young couple was active in every phase of Baptist life, and in August of the first year of their marriage they hosted, along with their small church, the annual meeting of Central Association, which lasted the better part of two days. In November they went to Las Cruces for the state convention. The president of the convention was Alma's father, Dr. C. M. Rock. Her mother led a devotional period at the WMU Convention; Alma served on the resolutions committee; and her husband presented the seminary report to the convention messengers and guests. They became part and parcel of every stratum of Baptist life and were supportive and faithful in whatever area they were asked to participate.

The *New Mexico Baptist Annuals,* over a period of many years, show that Mrs. Harry P. Stagg was a frequent pianist for Baptist functions, that she served on various WMU committees and programs, and that she received one dollar in payment in 1929 for travel expenses incurred as a state-approved Sunday School worker! Harry Stagg himself was quickly named to various committees; and as soon as the church in Gallup became self-supporting and he was thus eligible, he was named to the state Mission Board. He eventually became president of that executive body as well as serving concurrently as president of the New Mexico Baptist Convention. He was also president of the Montezuma Baptist Assembly, and in 1929 he gave a report on the state's assemblies. The people who attended these convocations were fed for an average of eight cents a meal that year, and the two-dollar registration fee paid for this cost as well as for their room and the program personalities' travel and honoraria! He reported no deficit!

On Easter Sunday, April 17, 1927, the Staggs were ecstatic over the birth of their first child, Lillian Carol. Named for Alma's mother, she immediately became the apple of her father's eye.

That Sunday the Gallup church sang and read Scripture and prayed without the gentleman from Louisiana!

By this time their car had been sold, and the work of the church was taken care of on foot. With the added care of the infant, Sunday mornings became a little hectic; and the father, persuading Alma of the need to be on time, became quite positive in his declaration that they must organize the procedures in such a way that they would be prompt. Alma announced that when he was ready for breakfast on Sunday, he was merely to say the word, and it would be laid in front of him. He could then eat and be relieved for his clerical duties, and she and Carol would come along as soon as they could.

On their first attempt at this new schedule, things seemed to be running smoothly. Breakfast was called for and eaten; dressing was completed; the preacher left for church. Alma finished dressing herself and the baby, walked swiftly to church, and taught her class. When she went solemnly in to play for the service, she noted that her husband had arrived without his necktie! Somehow she got his attention and apprised him of the situation. While the song service was being conducted, he slipped out and raced home for his absent cravat. Being on time to *anything* was never a subject of serious conversation again.

Sometimes it was absolutely impossible for the church to meet all its financial obligations, and the pastor's salary suffered accordingly. One year the family received only six hundred dollars of the twelve hundred budgeted for them. Alma substituted in the school system, and this often helped to tide them over. When this was inadequate, it seemed that God sent Elijah's ravens to sustain them! To depend on a flighty blackbird for the necessities of life seems almost foolhardy . . . *unless God sends the ravens!*

One day Harry was walking to the post office. His needs were great. He passed a picket fence which was heavy with intertwining vines. Nevertheless, his eyes fell upon something that didn't look like foliage. Stopping to pull it from the fence, he found a cylinder about the size of a pencil, began unrolling the tightly wound object, and found that it was two whole dollar bills! In those days a delicious hamburger could be bought for a nickel;

for another five cents, two hungry people could ask for an extra plate in a cafe and divide one-fourth of a tasty pie! Five pennies could be traded for coffee *and* donuts or could buy a whole quart of milk or a loaf of bread. He had found a treasure trove!

On a trip to Phoenix to visit the Rock family, Harry noticed a small object lying by the side of the road. (There are *thousands* of items along America's highways!) He was impressed to stop. He parked the car on the shoulder of the road and walked back to find a tightly rolled bill. When he opened it and saw the full treasure, he and Alma realized that it was a five-dollar bill, a ten-dollar bill, and a twenty-dollar bill! All Alma could think of was, "Oh, Harry, now we can buy the suit you so desperately need." And they could . . . and did.

Unexpectedly Harry was asked to perform a wedding ceremony for the daughter of a very wealthy family in the Gallup area. They had no connection with the Baptist work whatever; but when the minister arrived, he discovered that the groom was John Robert Gregg, originator of the widely used Gregg system for typing and shorthand. After the vows were completed, Harry excused himself and returned home. He then opened an envelope which Mr. Gregg had placed in his hands. It contained a crisp fifty-dollar bill, the largest remuneration for a wedding service Harry Stagg ever received in his entire ministry. For the rest of Mr. Gregg's lifetime, the Staggs received a Christmas message from him, mailed either from his New York home or his London address.

The two used their considerable talents and ingenuity, also, to augment their income. Alma sewed skillfully, making the clothing which she and Carol required, though the latter provided a temporary setback when she decided that her mother's one good dress didn't fit her needs for "dress up" and proceeded to cut it down to size! One cold winter Harry took his trusty .22 rifle and went hunting for rabbits. He shot twenty-five, almost all through the head, dressed them, and hung them along the back porch where they froze almost instantly. They made tasty eating for many meals.

One year Alma substituted in the schools every day, though

she was not under contract. At midterm she went to the school superintendent and asked him whether she would possibly be needed through the end of the year. "We need a car badly," she explained, "but it is impossible for us to get one unless we are assured of my teaching." He told her to plan for the car, but not before he jested, "You not only have to ask me whether you can get married, but whether you can buy a car!" He enjoyed taunting her about that for years; and the teasing formed a private, warm bond between him and the Staggs. They consequently found a Dodge car for about six hundred dollars, which helped them tremendously in their church responsibilities as well as transportation to school.

During all these activities, the war veteran was never without pain; and when he overexerted his strength he would have to rest and recoup his energies. He was under the perpetual care of doctors. In 1928 the pain in his nasal cavity where the gasses from the war had burned a hole in the cartilage became so severe that he had to have additional surgery. He and Alma and Carol left a concerned church behind as they went to Phoenix for the operation. After the medical procedures had taken place, Harry suffered excruciating agony in the healing process. At one juncture the doctors were not sure whether he would survive.

He passed the crisis one evening at the home of Dr. Rock, where he had been transferred from the hospital to recuperate. The telephone rang moments later; and Mr. Malone, the beloved deacon from Gallup, was on the line. "Mrs. Stagg," he said simply, "Brother Stagg is better, isn't he? And I can tell you the exact moment it happened."

Mr. Malone, owner of a little shoe shop, repeated his experience to the listening pastor's wife. He had been exceedingly uneasy about Harry all during the day. When he closed his shoe shop, he turned out the lights, locked the front door, and started to leave through the rear exit. But instead of going home, he knelt in the darkened shop and prayed for his gravely ill pastor until he had an answer. He went home to his wife, had dinner, and then called Phoenix, secure in his own mind that God had answered his prayers. Alma Stagg could only verify the truth already divinely revealed to that man of faith.

So close to death has Harry been, and for so many times, it seems almost as though he has led a charmed life. One day two friends invited him to take a plane ride. It was only a two-place craft. Just as Harry started to board, he was called to the telephone. Since he was away momentarily, his friends decided that they would take a short spin while Harry was occupied. The plane climbed briefly, then suddenly plunged into an intersection in Gallup. The wing cable had come off the spool, which controlled the tail of the craft. Harry conducted the funeral services for the two unfortunate victims.

While the church congregation was meeting in the courthouse, various visitors from all over the nation visited them since Gallup was a natural stopping place in a sparcely settled section. One such group was a deacon and his family from the First Baptist Church in Hollywood, California. They were on vacation and stopped long enough to worship in the improvised meeting house of the Baptist congregation. A few months later, Rev. Stagg received an invitation from the Hollywood church to be a guest speaker while their pastor was on vacation. Dr. Harold Proppe was the illustrious pastor of that church and had been for many years. Amazed at this unexpected request, Harry nevertheless accepted and prepared to leave for California by train. He left his struggling, much-loved congregation, and the one room with the crack chiseled by the earthquake. He bade his wife and daughter a tender good-bye and traveled to a different world.

Harry Stagg stepped into the most beautiful auditorium he had ever seen up to that time. The decor was tasteful, and every appointment had been obviously chosen with great care. He was humbled as he stood behind the pulpit where Dr. Proppe preached so effectively, and the spiritual atmosphere and general quality of everything he saw and felt was deeply moving. The deacons met with him for prayer before the morning and evening services. And outside, in lights eighteen inches high, his name appeared emblazoned for all to see. In his wildest imagination, the young preacher had never imagined his name going up in the lights of Hollywood! Between services he was royally entertained.

It was incongruous to him that he would be invited from a tiny church without even a building in which to meet and only partially supported by the state Mission Board to such a contrasting environment—in every sense. It was an experience for which he has always been grateful.

One of the strongest attributes of Harry Stagg has been his ability to make and keep friends from all areas of society, from different ethnic groups, and from various religious persuasions. When a young Italian woman was killed by her estranged husband and the Catholic priest did not wish to conduct her funeral services, her poor mother was distressed and didn't know where to turn. Another daughter questioned one of her Baptist friends at school. "What would your pastor do in a situation like this?" The friend, sympathetic to the family's dilemma, which only served to compound their sorrow, said, "I don't know, but I will be glad to call him and see if he will help."

The Italian girl was amazed and wondered aloud if the Baptist pastor would actually come to see them. After taking this possibility to her mother, the decision was made to call the friend's pastor. Brother Stagg went to the home and was welcomed by the family. He was greeted with tears of gratitude by the mother as she expressed to "Father Stagg" her relief and comfort at his presence.

The service was held in the home with several hundred in attendance. The overflow spilled onto the porch and into the yard. In Harry's message of comfort, the story of the cross was given and the plan of salvation was made plain. And during the rest of his contacts with the Italian mother she always called him "Father Stagg."

The Baptist minister was continuously called upon to conduct other funeral services for people who had no religious affiliation whatever. From as far away as across the border of Arizona they came and requested his help. On one occasion he went with the funeral director to the Catholic cathedral for the memorial services of a friend. After the service the funeral director told him, "I've had some trouble with my transportation. Could you take the priest out to the cemetery for the burial?" He gladly provided help in that unusual plight.

The Catholic people in Gallup were most gracious to the Staggs, and no doubt their generous spirit and their belief in the worth of all humanity helped to relieve some of the religious tensions often inherent in such extreme denominational stances. The Catholic hospital, the only one in Gallup at the time, provided physical and medical assistance when the Stagg family needed it. They allowed complete freedom of visitation at any time; in fact, the sisters would frequently call the Stagg residence to request pastoral care for the patients, including Catholics. One year when it came time for the important May Day celebration sponsored by the hospital and held on hospital grounds, Harry Stagg was invited to bring the main address. The next year he was asked to be the head of their financial campaign! This request obviously had to be declined. But the relationship was always open and cordial.

Because Gallup is the Indian capital of the world, colorful intertribal extravaganzas are held there each year. People from everywhere come, filling the hotels to capacity. Those fortunate enough to have friends there crowd in for the duration. The Stagg family entered into this celebration with delight, basking in the rich culture of the first Americans. They always had guests who seemed to add to the holiday air. Since the inception of this festival, they had ended their activities on a Sunday. Bravely Harry Stagg approached Gallup's civic leaders and laid before them a sincere request to move up their gala rites by one day. He pointed out the Christian observance of Sunday and sought their consideration. After some thought and discussion, they agreed to his proposal! He was delighted and grateful.

The Rocks came one year to view the ceremonials. There had developed a warm feeling of comradery between the two preachers, and each admired and loved the other deeply. Such visits between them were held whenever time permitted, and the trek to the arena was filled with anticipation.

The colorful, lavish ceremonial exploded before their eyes! They were enthralled as the program progressed, and Indians from everywhere in full, feathered regalia performed their ancient dances. At last the arena cleared, and one man rode before them in the firelight, seated upon a white horse. Brilliantly attired in his native Sioux costume, he opened his mouth to sing. There was an immediate hush among the thronging multitudes. And Dr. Rock, sitting in the excellent box seat arranged by his son-in-law, was mesmerized! The golden tones had been honed to perfection by the singer's extensive musical training. Affiliated with the Chicago Opera Company, the Gallup Festival was one of his many performances of the year. Dr. Rock began to covet, although he did not break one of the Ten Commandments!

Turning to Harry, Dr. Rock exclaimed, "I've never heard anything like that in my entire life! What a wonderful thing it would be for that voice to be dedicated to God! Do you think you could get an interview with him?"

Harry Stagg promised to try, and soon they were standing face-to-face with the talented young opera star. Dr. Rock, along with Harry, began to express their thrill and appreciation for his performance; then the older preacher added, "I covet your voice for God, and we are going to be praying for you that you will give it to him."

Later George Wilson, the Sioux with the velvet voice, said that his conversation with the two had struck him to the heart. He went to his room that night, but he could not sleep. He left for Albuquerque and couldn't sleep there either.

George was the featured attraction during the grand opening of the Kimo Theater in Albuquerque. His picture was in great evidence outside the motion-picture house. He made an impressive figure as he appeared in his authentic dress, and the audiences received him well.

As he was leaving the theater one day, a boy scout approached him, hoping to acquire some information for his scouting, but most of all wanting to take George Wilson to church! But when the boy extended such an invitation, George rebuked him rather roughly. The youth was not deterred, however, and insisted that they could go to his home until the service. George asked why the boy didn't grow angry when the answer he had been given was so harsh. The reply further convicted the singer of his need. "Because I am a Christian" was the lad's quiet response.

The unusual pair made their way to the boy's home and then on to the revival service, being held in the North Baptist Church (now Fruit Avenue Baptist Church). Reverend T. D. New preached a message that further stirred the heart of the gifted musician; and that night, when he could not sleep, he walked down the railroad tracks alone, seeking some solace. In desperation he sought a doctor to try to discover the source of his dilemma, but to no avail. He needed another Physician.

At last he went to Mr. New and poured out his agony. The preacher had the solution to the problems seething in his soul, and very quickly George Wilson turned over everything in his life to God. He asked for membership in that church, and immediately after his immersion sang from the baptismal waters "Jesus, Saviour, Pilot Me." He wired Chicago and told them that he was resigning his position with their Opera Company and would give his life to missions among the Indians.

This he did in a valiant way. Self-supporting at first, then receiving funds from sympathetic contributors, he was eventually employed by the Home Mission Board to work in the state of New Mexico. Baptists had not been able to have adequate witness among the Indians for many years; and his widow, in wonderful tribute to him, says, "He was the Lord's voice among the Indians after many years of silence." She also believes deeply that when young George Wilson was learning his first words of English in a tepee in South Dakota, the Lord was beginning to weave into the fabric of his life events that would lead him to the confrontation with Harry Stagg and Dr. Rock in Gallup. He always pointed back to their commitment to pray for him as the turning point in his life and considered Harry Stagg to be his spiritual father. He sang his way into the hearts and souls of people of all cultures and made a lasting impression on Baptist work in New Mexico.

He had promised God that he would serve him as long as he lived and as long as he could be helped to the platform where he could lean on the pulpit for support or could sing from a chair. His voice penetrated the airwaves and helped to engender faith and hope in his listeners. His theme song was entitled "Nor Silver Nor Gold Hath Been My Redemption"; and he sang it with deep feeling to the end of his days. Knowing that his days were numbered, he appeared before his last convention. Tired and weary and feeble of step, he was helped to the podium, where he sang:

> Precious Lord, take my hand,
> Lead me on—let me stand.
> I am tired; I am weak; I am worn;
> Thru the storm, thru the night,
> Lead me on to the light;
> Take my hand, precious Lord, Lead me home.

When he prepared for his own funeral service, George Wilson's request was that Harry Stagg preach the memorial message. In 1958, on Harry's birthday, the promise was movingly granted.

When God was ready to break his silence among the Indian people of New Mexico, he reached into a tepee in South Dakota and gave a golden voice to a little Sioux lad and arranged for him to be heard by the famous Madame Schumann-Heink herself and then to be taught by her. The doors of the Cincinnati Conservatory of Music were opened to him, and then he was trained further in New York. When he signed a contract with the Chicago Opera Company, the nation became his stage. But when he found the answer to life's greatest question and discovered that it had an eternal dimension, he knew where to invest his life.

During all these experiences Harry's major work, that of pastoring a church, continued. By the end of 1929 the membership

At work as executive secretary —Baptist Convention of New Mexico —in his own office.

was reported to be 103 with 179 enrolled in Sunday School. Thirty additions to the congregation in the twelve-month period served to accentuate the pressing need for more adequate facilities.

At last the corner of a hillside was purchased. A large ledge of rock protruded from the site. One man quarried this stone corner and stacked the stone nearby so that it might be used as the walls of the new church building. It was an exciting time as the design for the edifice took form. They decided on their most urgent needs and drew their plans accordingly. On one side of the auditorium they sketched in places for Sunday School rooms which could be made private by sliding doors and then opened as needed for added space in their auditorium.

Most of the work was done by the church members themselves as they gathered to build their new structure in the hole where the rocky hill had been. Alma Stagg joined in, nailing shingles, painting walls, and laying hardwood floors. She did not lay the stone . . . she couldn't even lift it! So thrilled were the people to have a house of worship of their very own that it didn't seem a hardship to construct it with their very own hands. To supplement the growing building, they bought mining houses for additional Sunday School space and placed them at the back of their property.

By doing so much labor themselves, a great deal of money was saved. However, it is interesting to note that the largest contributor to the First Baptist Church building of Gallup was a Roman Catholic businessman, a fellow Rotarian with Harry Stagg. After a period of six months of building, the congregation joyfully moved into their wonderful new place of worship.

The Great Depression in America was being felt in every quarter. Days of despair grew into weeks and months of despair as the choking hand of poverty dumped its victims into the turgid streets and highways of the nation, already glutted with human wreckage and dead dreams. The masses churned their way through endless soup lines. Tired, hopeless mortals shuffled through employment offices, taking up their belts another notch as they waited. At the back doors of homes across the nation were tapped tentative, reluctant, hungry knocks. People needed food. Mortgages went unpaid, and homes were lost. A banking panic began, causing a "run" on banks to extract deposits. On one day more than five thousand banks closed their doors. Newly made paupers jumped from penthouses to their deaths below, leaving behind worthless stocks and bonds and meaningless bank accounts.

As this woeful malady etched itself across the face of the earth, it left in its wake devastation which could not be erased. On the flood tide of massive hunger and joblessness, Adolph Hitler rose to power in Germany. Making the same empty promises of work and food in Italy, Benito Mussolini—Il Duce—was catapulted into world prominence and power. And in America, the New York governor who had worked out a system for the unemployed of his state won the first of four elections as President of the United States.

Immediately Franklin Delano Roosevelt began massive programs to alleviate the most pressing problems at hand. By providing bold work projects and pouring prodigious amounts of money into the seeming abyss, the economic maze seemed to lurch forward in gasps and spurts in its attempt to straighten out on its way to prosperity. And we forced to the netherland of our cerebral activity the haunting dirge that our taxes were higher and that our national debt was climbing.

Tragically, the Nazi and Fascist leaders capitalized on these vast human problems and began their aggressive march into war that was to change the face of Europe for all time to come. At last, because of the surprise attack on Pearl Harbor by the Japanese, the American President was left with nothing to do except declare war against that Oriental land on December 8, 1941; and our financial and human resources were poured into desperate fighting in two distant theaters of war.

The first institution to suffer from such financial turbulence and the last to recover seems to be in the area of the religious. In New Mexico there was mirrored the same weakened thrust found across the entire Convention. As gifts were diminished, so was outreach. In 1930 Montezuma College closed its doors, debilitated by indebtedness. The Baptist Hospital in Clovis was next. The corresponding secretary resigned, and he was replaced by a layman who worked for the paltry sum of one dollar a year. Missions suffered not only in the state but around the world—the Foreign Mission Board reported work in only thirteen foreign countries in 1934. Mounting indebtedness hung like an albatross around the neck of religious enterprise. Financial gimmicks and long-range plans began to emerge in an attempt to wrench part of what had survived from the claws of the giant monster.

Into this maelstrom Harry Stagg was drawn, and he found himself heading committees to study the Montezuma impasse or to examine the feasibility of electing a convention executive. As president of the convention, he was an ex officio member of various committees and was aware of needs as well as of funds available. Because he attended associational meetings and local functions, he was alert to the climate of feeling across the state.

A happy event broke into the solemnity of these difficult days when a second daughter was born to them. After almost nine years as an only child, Carol was joined by a sister on March 24, 1936. She was named Marcia Vaughan, bearing her maternal great-grandmother's maiden name. Sadly, her grandmother from Phoenix had died almost two years before Marcia's birth. Her parents had taken Mrs. Rock to San Francisco in the hope that a specialist there could suggest a cure for her. The doctor had been a friend of the Rock family for many years and had researched extensively in the field of Mrs. Rock's malady.

During the course of the tests and examinations on the patient, the doctor entertained the family in his home. While they were discussing various events of their lives, the doctor's French wife asked Mr. Stagg about his war injuries and where he had received treatment. When he recounted the story of the trip on the hospital train and the kind treatment he had received at the improvised hospital-hotel in Paris, she told him that she was a trained nurse and on that particular day had been in that hospital admitting all the patients who came into their care! Their paths had momentarily crossed sixteen years before under painfully different circumstances.

After Marcia's birth, Dr. Rock urged the Staggs to visit him in Phoenix so he could see his new granddaughter. Despite every good intention to do so as soon as time permitted, the Staggs were notified of Dr. Rock's sudden death less than four months after the new baby's birth. This has been a poignant memory for them, but it was one of life's sad moments which could not be reversed.

A well-deserved tribute was paid Dr. Rock in the 1936 convention that fall. He, along with his son Vaughan, who succeeded him at the Phoenix church, served Arizona Baptists for over fifty years; and from that church eighty-six churches and missions have been established. Another son, Thurston, served as pastor of New Mexico churches for many years and made significant contributions to the work of Baptists in the state.

As president of the convention, Harry Stagg moderated the business session where, again, the matter of securing a corresponding secretary was discussed. Three times the time was extended, but no conclusion for positive action could be reached. During the next annual meeting, Mr. Stagg was again elected president; and the convention instructed the state Mission Board to act in their behalf in the election of an executive officer. By this date, Gallup registered 185 total membership; the Lottie Moon Christmas Offering the previous reporting period was $1,769.16 (for the entire state); and about 11,000 members were reported on the rolls of 126 churches. The property of Montezuma College was reported as sold, and the funds from that sale were sent to the treasurer of the Southern Baptist Convention to apply on the college loans there.

Since the convention had instructed the state Mission Board to act in their behalf and to select and elect a corresponding secretary-treasurer, they set about the task.

The committee sat around a table in the headquarter's offices above the old Woolworth store. Harry Stagg, as president of the convention as well as the Board, was invited to attend as an ex officio member. After a period of prayer, the chairman asked that each member express himself as to the type of man they felt should be considered for that position. And they did so, one after another taking his turn. When they had finished, the man across the table from Harry lifted his finger and pointed it in Harry Stagg's direction and said solemnly, "You are the man."

The thought was so incongruous to the Gallup pastor that he burst into laughter. He said, "That is utterly ridiculous! I can't even give full time to my little church, and my wife has to do more than her share in order for me to serve at all. It would be utter folly for me to even think of such a position, with the need for travel and the difficulties of my physical problems. It is absolutely ridiculous! Utterly impossible!" When the rest of the committee agreed that the first man was right, Harry laughed at the entire group! He had never heard of anything so absurd. The difficulties of such a proposal conjured in his mind insuperable obstacles. He simply could not consider it.

They asked then if he would suggest someone. He offered the name of the pastor of the First Baptist Church in Roswell, Dr. Julian Atwood, who was held in high esteem in New Mexico. His many talents and attributes were laid before the group by Mr. Stagg, and the committee suggested they get in contact with him. They telephoned the hotel where Dr. Atwood was staying while in Albuquerque for the Board meeting, and he graciously consented to meet with them. They laid their proposition before him, and he allowed his name to be placed in nomination before the Board the next day. He was unanimously elected. But because this had been so unexpected to him, he asked for time to consider and pray about the decision.

The Staggs left for Glendale, Arizona, where Harry preached in a revival for two weeks. During this period Dr. Atwood notified Harry that he did not feel impressed to accept the position.

The preacher was completely exhausted; and as they started for home the next day, he was silent for a long period of time.

Alma, ever conscious of his needs, began to question him urgently about his feelings. "I know you've done too much," she worried. "What can I do to help?" She knew that it was not like her husband to travel for several hours in complete silence. And then he told her.

"I've been having quite an overshadowing experience," he related. "God has been talking to me, and I am in a real spiritual difficulty. He seemed to say, 'Now you laughed at that committee, but that is your job! When they asked you, you should have given their request serious, prayerful consideration . . . yet you laughed! This is your place of service; you can't evade it; you must do it.' "

As he shared with his wife the most overwhelming experience of his life, he told her that they would say nothing to anyone about his deep feelings; they would just pray, and if God wanted him in that position, he would accept.

When the Staggs reached home, he notified the committee that they would need another meeting. Although they had invited him to the first meeting, they met without him the second time. Because the group had to attend the Board meeting anyway, they met just before that convocation with the hope that they would have a candidate to present for election. During the Board meeting, Harry called on the chairman of that committee for a report. A name was presented, and it was time to vote. In unprecedented action, one gentleman arose and moved that they grant a five-minute recess. The Board agreed, and the standing member called Harry Stagg to a private area in the basement of the First Baptist Church where they were meeting. And he began to talk to the Board's president earnestly.

"I've prayed about this a great deal," he began. "I know in my heart that you are the man for this place; and if you will give your permission, I want to place your name in nomination." Harry asked, "Do you feel this with your whole soul?" The gentleman replied in the affirmative. Since he felt so strongly, permission was given, and they returned to the group.

The name of Harry Stagg was thus placed before the Board for nomination, and he and the other nominee left while the committee discussed the matter before them. When they returned, it was announced that Harry had been elected. This decision was deeply moving to the Gallup pastor; and when he was asked to make a statement, he related to them the experience he had been through. He told the whole Board that the committee had graciously offered him the position at the very beginning and that he had turned it aside as unthinkable. Dr. Atwood had declined, and then the conviction that he should have accepted the position came to him strongly. There was no need to ask for time to think it over or to pray further about it! He accepted on the spot.

He reminded them that there would be days when he could not function, that there would be appointments he would have to cancel. They were aware of all of these ramifications, but had elected him anyway! But because he felt so strongly about his work, he told them that since he could not give full time, he would not accept a full salary. Instead of accepting the three-thousand-dollar stipend, he would receive twenty-four hundred instead. This included no auxiliary benefits, but was acceptable to all concerned.

With a slender hold on his health, the Staggs moved to Albuquerque, not knowing how he could possibly meet the demands of his office. But if God was leading, he surely could follow.

And in January, 1938, the significant move was made.

VI. The Executive Secretary
PART ONE

It almost boggles the Western mind to consider that while Moses was leading the children of Israel through the desert to the Promised Land, there were others going about their daily business thousands of miles away in what would later be known as the Land of Enchantment. Indeed, some archaeologists and anthropologists put man in New Mexico as early as twenty thousand years ago! Records prove that when the earliest Pilgrims landed at Plymouth Rock, Santa Fe was already a bustling city. Today, as one visits a more modern city, there is little question that the flavor of antiquity rests heavily on the whole area as it lies protected in the valley formed by the last hurrah of the Rocky Mountains.

In 1539 the first Spanish horsemen came riding into the quiet pueblos. Resplendent in their bright regalia, they came seeking gold—and souls. The Spanish crown would have as easily sent their four hundred conquerors away without food and swords as without monks and friars to convert the people along the way.

The Indians, no doubt awed and mystified by their intruders, were rather easily overcome, and many were "converted." They believed that no spirit was a god over all and simply included Catholicism in their beliefs, adding one more spirit and the fetishes of the papacy. They gave nothing, and retained everything. When one visits the pueblos today, four hundred years later, one sees this same religious amalgamation.

Juan de Oñate, accompanied by colonists in long wagon trains followed by cattle, moved as far north as Santa Fe in 1598. They promptly built a church which claims to be the first place of worship in the United States. (A chapel in St. Augustine, Florida, also claims this distinction.) Immediately after their arrival missions were established in nearby pueblos. Twenty-two years later the first Pilgrims landed.

By 1717, however, certain religious leaders were preaching revolt from Spain. Although some were duly executed, the seeds of independence had been sown, and the resistance the revolutionaries inspired was such that until independence from Spain was finally achieved in 1821, their followers never wavered nor gave an inch. When Oñate had taken possession of New Mexico for Spain, he announced that it was for "God and King," thus marking the first union of church and state in America. For 310 amazing years, this theocratic monopoly went virtually unthreatened as Catholicism became increasingly entrenched in every facet of life.

In 1846, General Stephen W. Kearney of the United States Army occupied the New Mexico Territory, which then included Arizona, California, Nevada, Utah, southern Colorado, and parts of Texas, Oklahoma, and Kansas. Not a shot was fired. The General offered the first recorded word of religious tolerance heard in New Mexico as he spoke in Las Vegas.

Baptists of the Northern states sent Hiram Read to California as a missionary! After reaching Santa Fe, he used the opportunity to preach on the square. He was immediately invited to the Palace of the Governors, and the governor urged him to stay in New Mexico. Three prayerful days later Mr. Read gave an answer; he would stay. In 1849 Baptist work was officially opened in the state. He and Mrs. Read worked diligently and urged additional personnel. As more missionaries came, the work was expanded. (It was during this period, in 1851, that Archbishop Lamy came to Santa Fe from Europe. He is memorialized in the well-known book *Death Comes for the Archbishop* by Willa Cather.)

After the Civil War, unfortunately, Baptist missionaries were withdrawn from the state, and their properties were sold to the Presbyterians and Methodists. Eventually, in 1880, the work was resumed, although many of the earlier constituents had been absorbed by other groups. Ten years later, there were only 335 Baptists in the whole territory!

The first church to be organized was First Baptist, Las Vegas, in 1880. Raton followed the next year and Socorro in 1882. First Baptist, Albuquerque, was reorganized in 1887.

By the end of the century there were twenty-six Baptist churches in the state, none entirely self-supporting. The state university was founded in 1899, and the New Mexico Baptist Convention was organized in 1900. To head the latter, Reverend George Brewer was elected. A Board of Managers was set up as the official body for Baptists. (This later was changed to Mission Board and more recently to Executive Board by the enthusiastic passage of an amendment offered by Dr. Morris Chapman, pastor of Albuquerque's First Baptist Church, during the 1975 annual convention in Tucumcari, New Mexico.)

During this period, departments for Sunday School, Woman's Missionary Union, and Baptist Young People's Union were established. A Pastor's Conference was begun on an annual basis. Associations were formed, and by 1910 there were forty-one churches sending messengers to the convention. At that time a dispute over allegiance to the Northern or Southern Baptist Conventions arose to such a degree that a division occurred. For eighteen months there were two conventions, each claiming the whole territory; no amity agreement here! The Home Mission Board agreed to send the same amount of financial aid from the SBC headquarters as sent by the counterpart from the Northern Convention.

By 1912, the year New Mexico ceased being a territory and came into the Union, Baptists united and formed one convention once more, affiliating with the Southern Baptist Convention. Dr. E. B. Atwood was elected executive secretary, and three "Boards" were established: Missions, Education, and Philanthropies. The first issue of the paper, *The Baptist New Mexican,* had appeared three months before the convention had met. The growth was such that by 1915, 139 churches reported 6,341 members. In addition to the executive secretary and Sunday

School and BYPU workers, there were three regional leaders, three colporteurs, forty pastor-missionaries, and a Woman's Missionary Union field worker. There was no work among the Indians, and only three served the black race; five ministered to the Spanish.

The convention was chartered in 1917 for fifty years (and renewed in 1967). Dr. Atwood subsequently resigned to take another position and was followed by Dr. J. W. Bruner.

In 1918 there was no convention held because of the tragic epidemic of influenza. The Board met to take care of official business and agreed to the establishment of a children's home in Portales. The following year the seven thousand Baptists in the state accepted a goal of $250,000 for the Seventy-five Million Campaign!

Perhaps because of the aftermath of World War I, the ambitious financial goals for the Southern Baptist Convention in that endeavor were never quite reached by New Mexico or the Southern states. However, New Mexico was the first to go over the top in pledges and led the South in actual ratio giving, contributing $223,906 toward their pledge.

The valiant attempt to "religiously educate our children" in a higher place of learning was made when Montezuma College was founded in 1922. Plagued with financial woes from the first, it was eventually closed in 1930, leaving New Mexico Baptists with grievous debts.

When Dr. Bruner resigned, C. W. Stumph from Clovis was elected to succeed him. He served in many capacities during his years in New Mexico, and Baptists are forever in his debt.

In 1925, the year Harry Stagg came to New Mexico from Louisiana, there were fifty-five churches in the state without pastors; thirty-four pastors received state aid. One-third of the churches received state funding. And during that desolate decade, only thirty-five new churches were formed.

By 1931, when Mr. Stumph resigned, talk of indebtedness had become chronic all over the Southern Baptist Convention. As the depression dug in, it became psychological as well as economic. This was especially felt in the Southwest, where work was relatively new and reserve strength minimal. By 1933, when the budget of New Mexico's Baptist Convention called for $27,000, $12,775 was raised—the lowest since 1912! The host church for the convention the year before had announced that only messengers—no guests—could be entertained in their homes, so reduced were the circumstances of their members! Since Baptist hospitality has always been so liberal, one can understand the dire straits and the great poverty which prevailed. In fact, on a state level, the following adjustments had to be made during the years 1930-1935:

1. Withdrawal of pastoral aid (Home Mission Board could no longer continue this funding).
2. Employment of an executive secretary on $1 per year basis.
3. Sale or rental of Montezuma equipment.
4. Reduction, percentage-wise, of all bills where such reduction could be secured.
5. Closing of Montezuma Assembly.
6. Cessation of aid to ministerial students.
7. Elimination of printed annual (lasted 3 years); reduction of state paper to four pages.
8. Shifting of ethnic work to Home Mission Board *without* joint responsibility.

But "it was hard all over!" So pervasive had the depression become that it affected every area of life. People despaired of whether some degree of normalcy would ever return. The valiant attempts to hold things together during those desperate days cannot be overemphasized. Women turned the shirt collars for their husbands in order to make them last longer and painfully snipped the threads holding together their "best" suit, even turning it so the "shine" wouldn't be quite so obvious. And far from wondering why more was not done, one can only marvel that so much was done out of their penury. Marcia Stagg Cantrell remembers the poignant account of her mother's paying their tithe on a Sunday morning, well knowing that there was no food for the family's dinner and that there was no more money! But Marcia remembers that as they were leaving church that day, they were invited out to dinner!

And so the Staggs settled into their Albuquerque home; Harry began to operate from the Baptist headquarters. These offices were in an old frame building over Woolworth's store at the corner of Fourth and Central. There was simply a series of rooms with doors leading from one into the next and a door into the hall. The bookstore had the telephone! It was housed in a room approximately 12-by-14 in size. When one of the staff had a telephone call, he was notified through a buzzer system and had to thread his way through his office, down the hallway, and into the small book store. There was no office available for the new corresponding secretary-treasurer, so they rented a room overlooking Central Avenue which would suffice. However, it was across the hall and stairway from the other offices.

Immediately Harry Stagg began writing articles of encouragement in the *Baptist New Mexican,* using as a subcaption for many months "We Are Well Able—Let Us Go Up!" He announced goals, urged subscriptions to the Baptist paper, encouraged emphasis on evangelism, and appealed for increased giving. He related stories of churches he visited and reported on the Southern Baptist Convention as well as the meeting of the executive secretaries. He introduced new staff members and welcomed new pastors to the state. By October he was able to herald the good news that gifts were up all over New Mexico.

Interlaced among these activities was the urgent need and attempt to pay off the indebtedness of New Mexico Baptists and to get the financial affairs in order. Some of the old Montezuma bills ranged from Boston, Massachusetts, to San Antonio, Texas. An account in Denver, Colorado, had been made for coal on which $25 each month was paid. To the companies too far away to visit, Harry Stagg wrote letters assuring them of intent to pay and requesting understanding. But to businesses within the state, he made personal visits. The encounters were most pleasant when he was told, "We understand the situation and have long ago written the indebtness off; it's gone—you don't owe us anything." Others were equally gracious and wrote off twenty-five or fifty percent of the bill. Attempts were then made to pay these off regularly on a monthly basis. However, there were those who were extremely unkind and threatening. Undoubtedly the difficult days had so undermined their businesses that their frustrations were very close to the surface.

One man was particularly violent. After being told the nature of Mr. Stagg's visit, he erupted into a vindictive tirade as his visitor sat quietly and listened to the unbelievable virulence of that businessman. After the man's emotional fury had been spent, the preacher arose, excused himself, and said good-bye. A few weeks later another appointment was made, and Harry Stagg reappeared. The man was very subdued, apologized profusely, and received his guest most graciously. As a result, a splendid, most satisfactory adjustment was made on the bill. Several years later when Mr. Stagg was back in that city on church business, he was standing on a curb waiting for the light to change. Suddenly, without warning, someone slapped him across the back in warm, genuine greeting, but almost knocking him down in its intensity. When he turned, he saw that he was face-to-face with his businessman "friend" once more. They shook hands, and Harry was reminded of their encounters a few years back.

To the credit of the Baptist Convention of New Mexico is the fact that the money which had been sold for twenty-five cents on the dollar was repaid on the basis of one hundred cents on the dollar! It was only when a creditor's generosity and benevolence were extended that any less was paid.

During those years a layman, A. W. Hockenhull, meant everything to the financial confidence in which New Mexico Baptists were held. A banker, lawyer, and former governor, he lived in Clovis. He was on the state Mission Board and wielded a fine Christian influence in the state. When notes had to be made for the operation of the convention from time to time, the officials of the First National Bank in Albuquerque stated that any note with A. W. Hockenhull's signature on it would be honored. Through those crises-filled years, his signature often made it possible for Baptist work to proceed.

Late in 1938 it became necessary for the Baptist headquarters to be moved. An old building on Gold Avenue was found, located between Sixth and Seventh streets. This building had been used at various times as a residence, as an apartment house, and as a hospital! Certain readjustments were made, and the property was purchased. It was far superior to anything which had previously been occupied and gave valuable space for more convenient operation of the staff.

A basement was one feature of the "new" location. It had a very low ceiling. Even so, some equipment from the University Press was purchased which had been discarded by them and installed there. Baptists entered into their own press operation. Workers had to duck their heads every time they walked under the beams. But it was a start which led eventually to a very adequate printing operation. Due to the excellent management of this department, the cost of operation never exceeded fifty percent of any bid received for the same work.

There is a noticeable difference in the tone of the 1937 *Baptist New Mexico Annual* and the one which appeared in 1938. The reports were ecstatic over the seven new missionary pastors (up from three the year before), the five new churches, and baptisms up from 918 to 1,303. When, in 1939, the convention met in Clovis, their meeting was couched in the threat of war. However, the State Mission Board appointed a committee of twelve—nine pastors and three laymen—to study the Scriptures on tithing from "Genesis to Revelation." Their findings were then to be presented in a simultaneous study all over the state. They also resolved to "inform our constituency that any minister or deacon who does not consistently preach and practice tithing is unworthy of such an office as a leader of Southern Baptist folk." The committee was further charged to study scriptural assumptions of the church's responsibility toward the Cooperative Program and statewide means of spreading the gospel.

The results of this effort are staggering! After the study and training had been done through 1940 and 1941, it was reported that on the state level alone, the gifts had increased from $37,201.45 in 1941 to $67,006.17 in 1942! In 1943 gifts were recorded as $93,729.58. The next year the $100,000 mark was comfortably exceeded, and never again was there to be the

Off on a flying trip—Convention plane, Dr. Stagg, pilot.

agonizing terror of extremely short funding. Of course, gifts were increased at the local level as well, and the committees urged the study of Christian stewardship in each church in the state for at least one week each year. And although expansion was made possible in a more dramatic way and larger funding was needed as the cost of living index rose, there was no further mention in the state paper of only forty-nine percent of salaries being paid the headquarter's staff as occurred in 1939, or of cutting back in mission arenas.

In 1942 Harry Stagg thanked the churches of New Mexico for their tremendous response to the biblical method of stewardship and announced that all past due obligations were being taken care of. For the first time, Cooperative Program gifts exceeded the budget by $2,528.33. And the 1943 volume of *The Baptist New Mexican* carried announcement after jubilant announcement that "the Foreign Mission Board is out of debt; the Home Mission Board is out of debt; the Southern Baptist Convention Hospital is out of debt; the Baptist Bible Institute and Southwestern Baptist Theological Seminary are out of debt; and the Baptist Convention of New Mexico is out of debt!" This wonderful freedom pumped new blood and energy into the Baptist spirit. There was a desire to do more and to be more for the cause of Christ. In New Mexico alone the growth had been phenomenal; 25,575 Baptists were carried on the rolls of the churches, and 1,417 baptisms were registered.

With the closing of Montezuma College, there was no active and official presence of Baptist witness and influence on any New Mexico campus of higher learning. Through the years various committees were appointed to study the question of establishing a Baptist college. The debts from Montezuma, hanging over Baptists' heads for so many years like the sword of Damocles, were a nagging reminder of the intense cost of college support and served as a cautionary warning device. There was widespread belief that something should be done in this area; the challenge and obligation to youth is an emotionally charged issue. And well it might be; they are our tomorrow.

At last, Harry Stagg presented the philosophy which he felt

would be financially sound and yet would potentially reach far more youth than the establishment of one college. To establish a Bible Chair at each college or university seemed to be the most acceptable choice. Scholars who excelled in their fields could be employed to teach on these campuses and to organize some kind of student program. Since the question of church-state separation had to be dealt with, these activities could be cared for off campus, and accreditation could be given by another university and transferred to the New Mexico school.

Plans were worked out with Hardin-Simmons University in Abilene, Texas, for such accreditation and supervision. A goal of $25,000 was set for the first such building in Portales to serve Eastern New Mexico University students. As this money accumulated, it was invested in war bonds until time for construction.

In the meantime, Dr. C. R. Barrick was employed as the first Bible teacher and built his home in Portales, which was designed to care as adequately as possible for a student program and Bible teaching. Holding a Ph.D. degree from Southern Baptist Theological Seminary, he was eminently qualified educationally and theologically to fill such a position. His superior attributes inspired the desire to have on each campus a man who would have the same excellence in preparation.

When Dr. Barrick resigned to take a position in Albuquerque, Dr. A. L. Aulick succeeded him. Almost single-handedly he assumed responsibility for the financial campaign of the new Baptist Center adjacent to the campus and was a benefactor during that period as well as later, for he and his wife continued substantial gifts.

As a result of the successful program in Portales and the eventual occupation of a $75,000 Center, extensions were made in Las Cruces, Albuquerque, Las Vegas, and Silver City. The splendid teachers were employed and paid by the Baptist Convention of New Mexico but had to be approved by Hardin-Simmons University as well. Their credentials frequently matched those of the president of the institution they were serving. They were considered visiting professors, but even so enjoyed the status of those employed by the institutions themselves. They took part in the faculty meetings and were allowed to influence discussions and conferences. Their only inhibition, it seemed, was their inability to vote. They were highly respected and widely used in conferences and other fields ahd had a great bearing on the quality, tone, and spiritual life of these campuses.

The Center at the University of New Mexico was made possible by a memorial gift from Mrs. T. H. Rixey and her daughters of Clayton. Dr. Barrick came to Albuquerque to direct the planning of the new building, to become its first teacher, and to direct the student work for the state. Subsequently, functional and lovely buildings have been built for each of the schools mentioned above.

It was quite a blow when Albuquerque's city planners announced their intent to widen University Avenue. This would remove completely the beautiful Baptist Student Center so lovingly given and so widely used. Property around the university was exceedingly difficult to acquire, but Baptists were able to purchase land at the same location and rebuild once more.

As education "progressed" during more recent times, accreditation had to be sacrificed on all but one campus. However, the Baptist Student Union work continues. In retrospect, Harry Stagg only wishes that more could have been done at this level. Products from these classes are represented around the world today as they serve in places of need and responsibility. And he feels that some of the most sacrificial work ever done in the state was performed by these dedicated, highly trained teachers. Well qualified and competent to teach at much greater compensation, they nevertheless were committed to serve under reduced circumstances.

There is no real normalcy during a period of war; and when the bombing of Pearl Harbor occurred on December 7, 1941, the nation was plunged once more into the abyss of conflict. For several years the uncertainty of war played havoc with plans here at home. But even though there was an effect, it was not as devastating to the economy and to the human spirit as the

Great Depression had been. The nation was behind the effort to win on every front, and as the human drama of courage filled the newspapers from day to day, great pride tempered by heartache filled the American continent. In no way does this negate the tremendous sacrifice of young American blood or make light of families who suffered separation for long periods of time. But whereas the Depression had sown discord and despair, the war seemed to draw out the will to win and the heart to sacrifice. When the peace finally came in Europe and then in Japan, a nation couldn't have been more grateful or jubilant than the United States.

The next five years, 1945-1949, were for New Mexico Baptists a period of extraordinary expansion. An average of eleven churches was organized annually. Membership rose to 40,000 by 1949. The Baptist Foundation came into being, and the Children's Home and Inlow Youth Camp were expanded. Indian and Spanish work were enlarged. The Baptist Press was organized and took up the printing of *The Baptist New Mexican,* later adding *El Misionareo Bautista* for the Spanish Convention and *All-Indian Baptist* for the Indian groups. A Brotherhood Department was established, and Charles H. Ashcraft came to head that division. When the Evangelism Department began, Eual F. Lawson, then pastor of the First Baptist Church of Alamogordo, became its secretary. As has been mentioned, the BSU Department was established, and several centers were opened throughout the state.

During this period, it came to the attention of Harry Stagg that Hiram Read, the first Baptist missionary in New Mexico, had been buried in El Paso, Texas, in an unmarked grave. When it became possible, Mr. Stagg visited Concordia Cemetery and found by the grave numbers the resting place of one who had meant so much to New Mexico as well as to Arizona and Texas. The three state Baptist conventions then voted to erect an appropriate marker in honor of one for whom they held such high esteem. It stands there today, in silent tribute to a valiant pioneer missionary.

In 1946 Harry Stagg went to Abilene, Texas, and conducted the memorable revival for Hardin-Simmons University. He returned home to face major surgery, which required recuperation for several weeks. By August he was able to begin a partial return to his schedule. When the convention met in Hobbs in the fall, the WMU of the First Baptist Church presented lovely flowers to him. The messengers voted to send him to Copenhagen, Denmark, the following year to attend the Baptist World Alliance. (This he was unable to do because of an additional long illness.) They also voted to send him and two other representatives to Nashville for a meeting on the status of the proposed Western Assembly. They sent fraternal greetings to the Kansas Baptist convention, then seven months old.

The announcement was also made that New Mexico Baptists had reached their quota for world relief; in fact, they led the Southern Baptist Convention in percentage giving. They had registered 154 percent! They sent a resolution to President Harry S. Truman through Mr. Stagg applauding his stand on the separation of church and state. And they, for the first time, had exceeded two thousand baptisms for the previous year! When their executive secretary stood before them that year, he had served in his position longer than any previous man—nine years.

During the early part of 1947, in Harry's tenth year of service to the state, he endured a long, extended illness. The state Mission Board graciously gave him a six-month leave of absence, during which time he tried to recuperate. Others filled in for him in various functions. Two pastors, Philip McGahey and L. M. Walker, wrote articles in the state paper, keeping Baptists apprised of the numerous items of interest to them as well as of the condition of Harry Stagg. During this period, the matter of an assembly in the West was uppermost in his mind, and he seemed quite helpless to do anything about it.

By May, however, he returned to the office and picked up his work. He boarded a train in about the middle of the month for St. Louis, Missouri, where the Southern Baptist Convention was to be held. Several staff members went along also and saw to his welfare. However, before the Convention was over, his strength gave way completely, and he was helped back on a train and put to bed for the trip home. He was ministered to all during the trip to Albuquerque by the train's personnel. Surprisingly, when he reached home, his strength had been renewed sufficiently that he went right to work!

In June he appeared once more in Abilene, this time to receive an honorary Doctor of Divinity degree from Hardin-Simmons University. That Baptist institution has always had close ties with New Mexico, not only through its accreditation of college courses connected with student programs, but there are more New Mexico students enrolled in H-SU than there are represented from any other state except Texas. It was fitting that they honor Dr. Stagg in this manner because of the splendid record he had made in his work and for his influence and connections with that school of higher learning.

Not only was this a period of expansion and growth in New Mexico, but it was a time of testing as well. Several lawsuits were filed which unwittingly drew a Baptist voice into the courtroom.

One concerned Montezuma. While the college was in operation the leaders had sold some of the lots to individuals for residences. In the deeds was recorded the clause that the college would furnish them water and electricity at a nominal service charge. One of the purchasers defaulted on his payments and was foreclosed by his insurance company in Missouri. The company filed a $50,000 suit against the Baptist Convention of New Mexico, charging that it had not kept its promise to furnish water and electricity as stated in the deed. However, when it was brought before the court that the entire income of the state convention at that time was insufficient to run the power plant and pump the water, the court ruled that there was lack of ability to meet this demand and threw the matter out of court.

The next case did not directly concern the state Baptist convention, but encouragement and assistance were given nonetheless. The pastor at Lindrith, who was also president of the school board, was prosecuted for distributing religious literature in the public schools and for conducting the baccalaureate services of the high school in his church, at which time he read Scripture and led in prayer. For three days Dr. Stagg sat by his side in the courtroom and listened to the testimony and rebuttal. The judge asked the preacher to reproduce his sermon in court. The pastor went over it point by point. He indicated that there was singing, prayer, and Scripture reading. He gave him the gist of his sermon. At last, testimony was given that the Baptist church was about the only place adequate for such a gathering in the entire community, and the other accusations were very weak. Then the judge asked the bailiff to lock the doors and said that if anyone wanted to leave, he should do it then because no one would be allowed to enter or leave until the court recessed. Even though the judge himself was Roman Catholic, he proceeded to give a clear proclamation of religious liberty, the separation of church and state, and the ideals of Americanism. He completely exonerated the Baptist pastor and made strong statements as to the tremendous value of the religious and spiritual in one's education. He also discussed further the matter of community spirit and cooperation. This was an epochal case in New Mexico on the matter of religious liberty and the separation of church and state.

Early in 1948 a complete report was offered in the *Baptist New Mexican* concerning the Dixon case. Defendants as well as plaintiffs were named. Seventeen different localities throughout the state were charged with violating the principle of separation of church and state in the operation of their schools. Garbed teachers of the Roman Catholic Church were teaching in public schools and were drawing salaries commensurate with their training and tenure. The general public labored under the impression that such teachers did not receive such remuneration.

Further, it was alleged that books which were written primarily for use in Catholic schools had been purchased from state funds for use by these schools. They questioned the daily influence of religious pictures in the classroom and other religious insignia inside and outside of school buildings. They wondered whether or not tax-supported schools could legally be conducted in a building owned by the Catholic Church and charged that the children in these districts were, on a daily basis, subjected to sectarian or denominational religious training. Bus drivers were paid to transport such children to these schools.

As a result of these repeated indictments, the state superintendent of schools ordered an investigation. One appointee, however, was the director of the Catholic Church for the Archdiocese, while the other was reputed to be under the control of the same group! For a time matters went on as usual, even though the state Board of Education had advised the Archbishop that the hiring of sisters in the state of New Mexico was unconstitutional. The governor made certain admissions to the press but afterward refused to enforce the law he had sworn to uphold.

The teachers continued in the classrooms fully garbed and were alleged to require or encourage the study and learning of the catechism, requiring books of catechism and prayers to be kept in their desks at all times, and to hold regularly scheduled classes for Catholicism during school hours. Shrines and "holy" pictures were left in place; children were taken next door to the Catholic church for services and were encouraged to go to confession both during and after school hours. Reading charts were religiously oriented, and pictures were of a religious nature. Classes were opened with Catholic prayers, and children were required to kneel and make the sign of the cross. This occurred again at noon and at the close of school.

And so the struggle continued—a few religious libertarians against the hierarchy of the Catholic Church. It was painful to realize that those teachers who were sworn to poverty were doubly powerful: Not only were they wielding an influence in the classroom, but their salaries were being paid, tax-free, *to their religious order,* which in turn could finance court procedure for defense!

After several years of appeals and costly court actions, the matter was legally settled with full recognition of the Constitution of the United States as well as of the state of New Mexico.

Baptists in the state poured their efforts into this difficult case, and Dr. Stagg's energies and influence were used in this awesome fight for religious freedom. Dr. Myers, then editor of the *Baptist New Mexican,* wrote, "Religious liberty has been traditionally the work of Baptists. Where do we stand today when the matter rests directly at our door?" Typical of the Baptist stance, they stood for complete separation of church and state and supported the case financially as well as morally.

Because of the growth of Baptist work in the state and the expansion of the staff, the building on Gold Avenue began literally to burst at the seams. It became obvious that a building specifically designed for their use was a necessity. As a result, it was arranged that land would be purchased for the eventual erection of a new building. But because of New Mexico Baptists' active pursuit of the Western Assembly and their need to buy property at Glorieta, the land was later sold for double the purchase price. This heavy involvement (explained in chapter 8) thus delayed the acquiring of adequate facilities for several years. But at last the state Mission Board voted to proceed with the plans.

Dr. Stagg still remembers vividly that meeting. A banker walked up and down the aisle of the room in which they were meeting, talking as he paced. He went over the whole situation carefully. He outlined in detail everything they would need on the basis of the contracts just approved. Certain cash on hand would be needed, and options were given as to the arrangement of the balance. "His assessment," Dr. Stagg recalls, "was not even a first cousin to our proposition. From a banker's point of view, what we were proposing was impossible, completely unrealistic." But the banker completed his speech with the words, "If Harry Stagg believes we can do it, you have my vote!"

Land had been acquired on Central Avenue, and the staff was requested to figure space adequate for their immediate needs as well as for future expansion. The plan called for enough space to be rented for offices so that these funds could be used to pay on the note of the building.

In addition, there had been a promise of a $50,000 memorial gift to be used specifically for the headquarters building. This had been fully counted on in the original presentation to the Board and figured into their approval of the contracts being let. Sadly, however, there arose legal complications which appeared to be insurmountable. A little Indian girl who lived on a reservation had been legally adopted by the generous couple before the death of the husband. All moneys from their estate would be legally tied up until the child became twenty-one years of age!

Matters looked extremely bleak! Discussions were held with the family representatives, their lawyers, and the attorneys representing the state Baptist convention. The result was a complete deadlock. Dr. Stagg requested an interview with the lawyer representing the family and was refused. "There is no way," the attorney said, "for any money from that estate to be released as promised. It is irrevocably sealed."

Contracts for the building had already been let on the strength of the original pledge. The widow, however, graciously agreed for Dr. Stagg to accompany her the next time she sought counsel from her attorney.

When that meeting occurred, Dr. Stagg walked into the lawyer's office with the lady. Although shocked, the lawyer greeted him, and they exchanged a few brief comments. But then, growing serious, the attorney said, "I wrote you that it was unnecessary for you to come—and I meant it. We have business to take care of. I will give you four reasons why this money cannot be released, and then I will excuse you."

After relating his reasons precisely, Dr. Stagg asked whether the man would give him a moment to reply to each statement. The request was granted, whereupon Dr. Stagg proceeded to discuss them point by point. When he had completed his explanation, the lawyer apologized for having written him as he had done, as well as for receiving him as he had. "There are some things about your organization and operation of this commitment that I did not know. And since I did not know your organization functioned as you have described, I will consider the matter further and will subsequently make a recommendation to the district judge."

When Harry Stagg had left home in an attempt to secure money for the down payment of the building, he did not know how far his search would take him. If the attorney had not been cordial, his plans were to drive to Dallas and perhaps to Oklahoma City for funding. He took his daughter Marcia along because of his physical frailties and told his wife when he left that he would not return until the money had been made available by some means. He simply left with his young child, trusting the Lord to provide a way for a purpose which he felt was so right.

Buoyed by the lawyer's consideration, they returned home. Within a week or so the district judge allowed enough money to be released that the crisis was averted, even though the amount originally promised was not available; nor was it ever forthcoming.

It was a happy day when the building was occupied in 1951, late in the year. It carried the memorial plaque in honor of Mr. R. L. Brunson, whose widow had made available all the funding she could legally muster. At the time of its erection, it was one of the most adequate headquarters buildings in the Southern Baptist Convention and met with considerable accolades and congratulations. Costing $200,000 and of Spanish-colonial design, it has housed the offices of the convention staff as well as the Baptist Press and the Baptist Book Store. The property on Gold Avenue was sold to the previous owner for double its purchase price.

"That building was a miracle," Harry Stagg muses today. "We really paid for it many times because we used it as collateral for additional loans when student buildings were needed."

It is heartwarming to realize that not only has the building been functional during these twenty-five years, but it has been used as a means for the expansion of God's work in New Mexico.

VII. The Executive Secretary
PART TWO

Late 1951 and early 1952 found the Staggs touring twenty-seven countries in Europe and the Holy Lands. In appreciation for their fifteen years of service, the state convention voted to send them on such a trip in order to "challenge us to the world-wide need for the message of Christ." Marcia accompanied her parents, who cared for her expenses.

Dr. Stagg wrote from their various locations, and these articles appeared week by week in the *Baptist New Mexican.* Repeatedly he expressed gratitude for the trip and for the new vision and sense of purpose he was experiencing. They spent Christmas Eve in Bethlehem and viewed the heavens from the shepherd's field. He preached in Cana of Galilee and in Nazareth. Besides viewing the poverty of the refugees in the new nation of Israel, they awoke to the cry of the muezzins in Damascus, which called the Moslems to the first prayers of the day. They crossed over into the Hashemite kingdom of Jordan, where many of the holy places of Palestine were located. They saw the marvels of Egypt and the grandeur of Europe.

Everywhere they went, the need of the gospel was apparent; and Dr. Stagg, seeing this urgency, wrote, "We will have a new life." This new insight was reflected in his message to the Woman's Missionary Union Convention that fall when he proclaimed, "The only way to exalt Christ in New Mexico is to do this worldwide."

In the summer of 1952 the excitement in New Mexico was contagious as preparations were made for Pioneer Week at Glorieta! Dreams of a Western Assembly were coming into fruition, and the list of Baptist leaders appearing on that first program is most impressive. Harry Stagg's name is on that roster, and later in the year he wrote an article for the Baptist paper which outlined a dream which still has yet to be realized. In his mind's eye, he envisions hundreds of foreign-exchange students converging on the Glorieta grounds on an annual basis. These students representing countries and religions from around the world would enter American life briefly for an education and then return to their native lands.

"How wonderful," Dr. Stagg enthuses today, "if they could be at Glorieta, rubbing shoulders with the giants of business and industry and religion. They could have conferences in their fields of training from representatives sent to Glorieta by their huge corporations. They could also meet the potential leaders from their own countries and from nations around the world. Religious services could be held on a volunteer attendance basis. I see it as a wonderful opportunity to witness to these students in a purposeful manner."

During the years of Dr. Stagg's service as executive secretary, the transition of Spanish and Indian mission work from the exclusive direction of the Home Mission Board to a joint agreement and direction with the state was made. The study, evaluation, and research was carried out by the Home Mission Board and Dr. Stagg. Programs were then set up to seek to accomplish the evangelization and training of these ethnic groups. This combined program gave the state its rightful share in financing and directing all areas of the work. This ultimately led to the establishment of work among the black community. Gradually all of this mission work was brought closer together in a more unified manner and had a greater impact in the local churches and associations. This growth eventually made necessary the organization of a Missions Division in the state.

In an attempt to lay the groundwork for the coming of a new superintendent of Baptist mission work, Dr. Stagg visited an Indian pueblo. The people listened attentively as he told of the many qualifications of their new Baptist leader. When

Arrival at Tinian; Navajo hogan on left and Indian trading post in rear. Plane taxied up for "curb service!"

he had finished, an elderly man arose and said, "That may all be well and good, but will he love us Indians?" He had immediately found the common denominator to all of our work for God: love.

Another day found Dr. Stagg as the mediator in a disagreement in one of the Indian churches. The man in charge attempted to present the church's position, but another member was of a dissident view. At last the moderator took a stick and drew two lines at right angles to each other. Pointing to the closed tip of the figure, he addressed the disgruntled man. "Walk these lines," he requested. Starting at the point of the angle he took two or three steps and then could take no more. Standing with his feet wide apart, the leader spoke to him: "Now, walk with us." The point was made, and the impasse was settled graphically.

When Dr. Stagg sought to open work in Navajoland in the Four Corners area, he met with great resistance from the tribal chief. Dr. Stagg told him of the opportunities which could be afforded their children through a Christian ministry. Still there was no favorable response. At last the chieftain did an about-face. "Our young people have to be shown a different way of life," he agreed, "and if you will build a building, we will give the land." Since all reservation and pueblo land belongs to the Indians, there is no way to build a church without permission. This was a great victory, and immediately missionary Louise Mitchell took a mobile home to the area. By the time a church building had been erected, she had visited every place possible. Everything had been made ready for the establishment of a mission. The work is still in operation today.

The work among these groups expanded to the extent that today over one hundred missionaries serve across the state and make a marvelous contribution to the cause of Christ in their own regions as they speak and communicate in local churches and in other states as well.

Harry Stagg's interest in the physical well-being of people goes back to his early childhood days, when he first accompanied his doctor-friend on the rounds made in the old buggy. His call to medical missions had to be averted because of his own physical maladies, but undoubtedly the suffering he saw during his years as a soldier added to his desire to alleviate pain. His close association with the hospital and the doctors in Gallup was an outgrowth of this interest. And when he considered the remote northern part of his beloved state, the yearning desire to try to meet needs there came to the fore.

At that time, roadways were almost nonexistent in that area; many people were extremely destitute, and infant mortality there was the highest in the United States because of the lack of medical facilities and the general rural deprivations. An exploration of the location suggested a situation very similar to that which is found on some foreign fields. After a careful analysis was made, a site was chosen which was in the center of many of these small communities, where the medical help would be most accessible to the greatest number of people.

The Baptist convention was most fortunate in being able to secure the services of Dr. and Mrs. E. K. Bryan, returning missionaries from China. Dr. Bryan was to set up the medical clinic and to minister to those people who were almost entirely without medical care. An old house had been renovated for the use of the clinic, and another was purchased for the residence of the missionaries. Necessary equipment was installed for medical care and treatment; later an ambulance was purchased for use in that remote area to transfer patients to distant hospitals.

The Bryans, although accustomed to the full financial backing and funding from the Foreign Mission Board, did a tremendous job under the most difficult circumstances.

When the Bryans moved away, they were followed by other doctors who worked most effectively. After several years of service to that area, other medical help became available which was partially adequate. Roads and highways were built which made travel to a hospital possible, and the Baptist clinic at Park View was closed. However, the record shows that infant mortality had dropped impressively, and the level of life had been raised for many. The Park View Baptist Medical Clinic had filled a tremendous need.

In 1918 the First Baptist Church of Portales began a children's home with four children and a matron to care for them. As the project grew, the offer was presented to the state Mission Board to accept this endeavor on a statewide basis. In October, 1919, the Board agreed to this proposal. Forty acres of improved land known as the Dr. Baily Place had been secured. This property boasted two thousand fruit trees, a modern bungalow, and a pumping plant. Within six months there were twenty-one children in the home, and need for expansion was great. This took place slowly as numerous matrons and superintendents cared for the children and property over the next several years.

In 1937, while Harry Stagg was president of the state Mission Board, the Walker C. Hubbards were employed to conduct the affairs of the Home. He took care of business management and procedures, and she served as the much-loved matron. Their service was so complete and held in such high esteem that when they retired in 1971 after thirty-four years of valuable contribution to children and to Baptists across the state, they were among the group to whom the annual was dedicated. During those years, subsequent land purchases for the Home made possible other acreage from which they could operate. Buildings were added to serve the children more effectively, and endowments were made through generous benefactors. Dr. Stagg secured many of these financial considerations but credits the Hubbards with the major thrust and growth of the Home during those important years of expansion.

Another important interest to New Mexico Baptists was the beginning of Inlow Youth Camp. When the ladies met in the Sandias in 1938, they requested that each camper appear with her own week's sustenance: $2.50 in cash, two cans of corn, two cans of tomatoes, two cans of peas, two cans of milk, one box of spaghetti, one pound of bacon, five pounds of potatoes, two pounds of sugar, one dozen eggs, and one dozen oranges! By 1940, however, the women of the state had found a possible location for a permanent camp in the beautiful Manzano Mountains; and with the approval of the state Mission Board, they had purchased the site.

A request went out from the WMU Office that each woman in the state set aside ten cents per month in order to meet the payments on the property. Named for Miss Eva Inlow, state WMU director for twenty-five years, the camp is one hour away from Albuquerque and almost in the geographic center of the state. The summer days are warm at the 8,400-foot elevation, and the nights are delightfully cool. The mountain slopes are covered with pine, pinon, cedar, spruce, fir, and aspen trees; and their tantalizing odor fills the air. The main lodge had served as the home of the owners of the Sun Valley Ranch and today is the headquarters for the camp as well as for the residence of part of the staff. A tabernacle, a first-aid station (the Pill Box), a dining hall (Manna Hall), and numerous log cottages have been built to serve the campers.

In all of this building and maintenance, Dr. Stagg played an active and supportive role. In regard to his help, Miss Inlow wrote, "He helped work out the plan whereby Woman's Missionary Union (unincorporated) could and did purchase and pay for the property that is now known as Inlow Youth Camp. After the purchase, he advised and helped with every plan, every new building or improvement, including water, electricity, telephones—his helping hand was never once withheld; nor was his presence at camp when he was needed."

Through the years thousands of people have enjoyed the benefits of Inlow Camp. Numerous missionaries from around the world state that their first impressions of the needs of humanity came to them during their days at camp. And wherever one goes in the state, there are people who are serving in full-time or lay capacities because of the commitment to serve during their days at Inlow.

In 1959 the Baptist Foundation was established as a separate division, and a full-time director employed. When asked whom he would suggest as a director, Dr. Stagg replied, "I know just the man. He is a native of New Mexico; he taught at Hardin-Simmons University for many years; he came to New Mexico all during those years to speak in behalf of his school and influenced many to seek their educations there. He knows New Mexico and its people like the back of his hand. . . . He is W. C. Ribble."

The committee then asked Dr. Stagg to contact Mr. Ribble, who at that time was serving Ouachita College in Arkadelphia, Arkansas. When Mr. Ribble answered the telephone and Dr. Stagg related his mission, the startled man replied, "I am looking at architect's drawings right now of a home we are planning to build. The contractor should be starting very soon on the construction." Dr. Stagg urged him to consider the request prayerfully. At last word was received in Albuquerque that the new house plans had been stored away . . . that God seemed to be directing them to come west. And Dr. Ribble served in that position most effectively for eleven and one-half years until his retirement in 1971. The Foundation, previously in combination with the Brotherhood Department and then with the Stewardship Department, was firmly established during Dr. Ribble's tenure.

During these busy years, Mr. H. C. Reavis served as manager of the Baptist Book Store. He had served the Baptist Convention of New Mexico in many capacities and for many years. Through the difficult period of the depression when there was no executive secretary, Mr. Reavis did the work of one as well as conducting many of the financial affairs of Baptists. Evelyn Denby, a co-worker through many of these years, served as bookkeeper, assumed administrative functions for the book store, and did typing for the staff when no secretary was available to them. Whatever needed to be done, she capably took hold and did it. In tribute to Mr. Reavis, Dr. Stagg says, "He made as large a contribution as any one in the state. He made untold sacrifices; there was nothing that he didn't give his whole soul to in this state. And the Board passed an important resolution in recognition of him and his valuable work in New Mexico."

In the middle 50s Dr. Stagg led a group on a mission tour through Mexico and Cuba, visiting our missionaries along the way and gathering information which could be effectively translated into action once they returned home. He visited Dr. Herbert Caudill in Havana, who later, along with his missionary son-in-law, David Fite, spent several years incarcerated in Cuban prisons as "guests" of Fidel Castro. This visit gave Dr. Stagg a valuable insight into the hardships through which our neighbors to the south were passing.

In 1963, at the invitation of the Foreign Mission Board, Dr. Stagg returned to Germany to conduct several revivals in churches serving English-speaking people. Near the location of one of the meetings was an Air Force base. The commander of the hospital was Dr. Stagg's nephew, a flight surgeon for over twenty years. When the church responsibilities had been completed, the nephew entertained Dr. Stagg in his home and then took him on a memorable tour of the battlefields of France where the veteran soldier had fought forty-five years before.

Some of the old barns where he had sought refuge from the terrible cold of winter were still standing and recognizable. Many of the villages had been partially destroyed, but those still remaining were poignantly remembered. Harry Stagg was able to outline in his mind certain trenches and battle emplacements where he had been. These areas had not been put back into cultivation, but were used for pastures at that time. It was a deeply moving experience to him, and his nephew took pictures which are still greatly treasured. They had lunch at the Officers' Club in Nancy, which had been their regimental headquarters for some time. They spent the afternoon visiting other towns where battles had been waged and viewed the fortresses; they had dinner in Verdun, where so many shells had come over American trenches.

Many memories welled up in his heart and mind, conjuring up deep experiences of the past. But one reaction was a surprise to him. In Germany, while visiting some of their national cemeteries, a strange feeling overwhelmed him. Lying buried before him were countless thousands of men who had opposed the Allies during World War I. They had been the enemy, to be overcome at all costs in order to preserve American freedom. He read their markers, noting their names, their numbers, and regiments. And doing so made a difference in his thinking.

There were memorials to sacrifice on the other side of the war! They had suffered excruciating heartache, too. And while his major thoughts had always been to the damage, destruction, and devastation to his own side and to the sorrow and trauma to the American people and her allies, a new realization of the agony of others shook him to the core. The only comfort he could realize at all was to remember that America had not been the aggressor; we had to defend our country and our way of life.

Sentiment had begun to develop by people in the southern part of the state for a camp to be established nearer them. They felt that they would be able to use such facilities more frequently and in greater numbers if transportation was easier. Also, for a long period of time, the road to Inlow Youth Camp often made travel difficult. As this interest developed and grew stronger, such a need was met. Today Sivells Baptist Camp, high in the Sacramento Mountains—but accessible by a good highway—serves an important need in caring for camping programs. The initial outlay of money and financial burden has been offset, Dr. Stagg believes, by the success of the new provision.

Named for the Brotherhood Secretary, Dr. H. C. Sivells, the beautiful property cost $29,000. It includes 160 acres of land near Cloudcroft. Gradually various units were constructed to meet the needs of the men and boys who would attend. Crafts of all kinds are provided, and hiking trails are well trod. On July 4, 1964, during Pioneer Week, people from all over the state were invited to come to a barbecue and to attend dedication services. Since that time, the mountains have reverberated with the joyous experience of Baptists converging on that spot.

During all these years of promotion and expansion when the Bible Chairs were established on five campuses and buildings erected, when the Glorieta dream was being realized, when huge indebtedness was paid off, when the new Baptist headquarters building was being erected and the staff expanded, as the growth of mission sites and missionaries occurred all over the state, as the children's home grew and developed and Park View Medical Center was developed in Chama Valley, Harry Stagg carried on his "normal" work load. He represented New Mexico Bapists in meetings in many places of the world and on various boards and defended them in the courts of the land. He carried a heavy speaking schedule, as he was in demand when new church buildings were dedicated, at state conventions, in local churches, and for revival meetings.

Harry administered the work of the convention and bore its many burdens for three decades. When Mrs. Stagg could, she accompanied him, although for twenty-five years she served as teacher of math for the Albuquerque Public School system. And in 1966 he announced his retirement!

On hearing this report, however, an objection developed spontaneously from all over the state, urging him to stay until the completion of a full thirty years. This would involve an additional sixteen months of service.

When the state Mission Board met in Albuquerque, Dr. William D. Wyatt, pastor of the First Baptist Church in Albuquerque, presented a recommendation to the members gathered. He told them that pastors and laymen from all over the state were strongly urging the Board to ask Dr. Stagg to remain longer in his position. The Board unanimously voted to make this request of him and, furthermore, appointed a committee to set up goals which might be reached before his retirement.

Dr. Stagg was not present for this time of discussion, and when apprised of their request, said simply, "This is one of the greatest honors and compliments you could bestow upon me following twenty-eight years in this position . . . I do not know of anything in all the world that my heart is in as much as the work of this convention." He stated further that he could not give them an answer until he had a physical checkup. He anticipated no problems, but simply wanted to be as certain as he could that he would be able to serve for the additional period without encountering health difficulties.

When he gave his answer, it was a welcomed "Yes." And the editor of the *Baptist New Mexican,* Horace Burns, enthused, "For two years ahead of us we may anticipate his vigorous leadership, challenging goals, and new achievements as we rally not merely to the leadership of our beloved and respected leader, but to the call of God and the challenges of the day in which we live . . . The Baptist people of our state have every reason to rejoice and to have some feeling of pride—not just that Dr. Stagg has served so long, but that so much has been accomplished."

A few months before the retirement period, Dr. R. Y. Bradford was chosen as "executive secretary-treasurer-elect." He was to serve with Dr. Stagg for two months in order to become acquainted with some of the procedures and policies under which he would work. And the gift of two months of terminal leave during December and January (1967-1968) completed the tenure of Harry Perkins Stagg in New Mexico.

When twelve hundred friends, relatives, messengers from the state, and Southern Baptist leaders converged on Hoffmantown Baptist Church for the service honoring the Staggs, it was the forty-first consecutive state convention which he had attended. The records state that there was a "gigantic eulogy" as people from all over the United States gathered to pay tribute to thirty years of valuable service and to the quality of the man and woman who had rendered it. Thurston Rock spoke for the family; Joseph Underwood, a former staff member, spoke in behalf of the Foreign Mission Board; Bernice Elliot, a former staff member, spoke in behalf of Woman's Missionary Union in Birmingham. Eual Lawson, also a former staff member, paid tribute in behalf of the Home Mission Board; Porter Routh spoke for the Executive Committee of the Southern Baptist Convention; and James L. Sullivan represented the Sunday School Board. Jeff Rutherford represented the current staff of the New Mexico

Baptist Convention.

After these generous tributes, Harry Stagg was presented and received a standing ovation. Then he addressed his beloved co-workers for the last time as their leader. Mr. Burns wrote, "He held the audience spellbound as he traced the development of Baptist work in the state over the past thirty years and then outlined possible growth for the future."

A few days later his name was taken down from his office door and replaced with the new leader's name. His books and the accumulation of thirty years were carried from the Baptist headquarters building. He met with the much-loved and valued staff for a final devotional period. He walked down the steps, carrying the weight of his seventy years very lightly, and opened the door to a new day.

One would hope that he remembered the letter received just days before from his dear friend, Dr. James Bryant, former Executive Secretary of the Baptist Convention of Virginia, who wrote: "You have so much to rejoice over and so little to weep over."

VIII. The Visionary

When one glides along the beautiful Pan-American Highway (Interstate 25) south and east of Santa Fe and thrills to the sight of Glorieta Baptist Conference Center nestled in the stately Sangre de Cristo Mountains, there is no hint of the drama or the sacrifice which went into its realization. But the story of Glorieta is one of the most appealing sagas in Southern Baptist life. Because of the active role of Dr. Stagg in this regard, the account is given here.

While his father-in-law, Dr. Rock, was pastor in North Carolina years before, he had been active in the establishing and development and promotion of Ridgecrest Conference Center (formerly Assembly). He built a summer cottage there which is still in use by the conference center. No doubt the value in which Ridgecrest was held for the development of Baptist leaders made a deep impression on Harry Stagg.

As trips were made from great distances to Ridgecrest, the idea began to simmer for such an assembly in the western mountains. Although the beauty and training at Ridgecrest were deeply appreciated, there were multitudes of leaders from western areas who could never appropriate its help because of the length of the trip. The Sunday School and Training Union Secretaries from the various states perhaps felt this urgency first, followed by pastors and other denominational leaders. It became a subject of discussion in various group meetings, and interest became widespread.

During these years Dr. George W. Truett preached annually at the Paisano Baptist Encampment in West Texas. There was some strong support to develop this site into a Western Assembly because the strong, inspirational preaching of Dr. Truett had brought considerable attention and renown to that area.

When the Baptist General Convention of Texas met in Mineral Wells in 1945, a group of interested pastors and laymen met in their hotel to discuss the possibility of an assembly in the West. All present were of the opinion that representatives from the surrounding states should meet with them at a subsequent time for discussion. Therefore, a meeting was called for this purpose in Dallas, and invited representatives from Oklahoma, Missouri, Arkansas, Louisiana, and New Mexico attended. From New Mexico Dr. Stagg and Mr. W. J. Lites came, the latter being the Sunday School Secretary for his state.

As the discussion began, the Texas representatives felt that Paisano should be supported; the Missourians suggested Hollister Hill. Dr. Stagg and Mr. Lites felt that the assembly must be located farther west because of the expansion of Baptist work to the Pacific Coast and in the Northwest. "Why build another assembly which would serve the West unless it is located centrally in the West?" they questioned. A Mr. Kokernot from Texas, a multimillionaire, was extremely interested in the Texas offer and implied that a significant gift would be forthcoming from him. Dr. Stagg, sitting next to him in the circle, asked him if he would be willing to make such a gift if the assembly were located in another state. Mr. Kokernot graciously agreed that such was his intention. Unfortunately, he died before he had made provision for such wishes to be carried out.

Dr. Stagg then injected the idea of a winter program. He thought of places such as Sun Valley and Aspen, Colorado, which offered wonderful opportunities for winter sports, and wondered aloud why Baptists couldn't and shouldn't provide winter training as well as summer. It was a completely new idea in denominational thought, and they dreamed of ice-skating, sledding, skiing, and campfires for the outdoorsmen who could combine recreation with their classes. But the idea was quickly passed over by the majority of the group. Dr. Stagg, however, continued to feel that such an outlay of capital, coupled with the need for training, should be on a year-round basis.

When the group adjourned, it was agreed that the matter would be brought to the attention of the Southern Baptist Convention, which would meet in Miami, Florida, the following June, 1946. During the intervening months, those from the group wrote letters, made speeches, and generally promoted the idea of a western assembly. Various sites were suggested, and warnings were signaled concerning moving so far out West as New Mexico—then the fringes of Baptist work. It was inconceivable to the majority of Baptists at that time that the expansion in the West and Northwest would be as rapid as it has proven to be. Dr. Stagg, however, had seen his own convention double in membership in the previous decade; and this expansion seemed a harbinger to him of growth to come. A growing sense of the rightness of an assembly in the rugged Western mountains took hold of him. He never lost a sense of commitment to that mammoth task, even though he could not know at that time the tremendous sacrifice, disappointments, frustrations, and cost required of him and New Mexico Baptists.

When the Convention met the following year in Miami, they voted to appoint a special committee to study the feasibility of establishing a western assembly. The president, Pat Neff, understood that he was to appoint the committee and did so. The Executive Committee of the Southern Baptist Convention thought that it was their duty and also appointed a group. After some discussion, the two decided to merge and work together.

In the South there was considerable feeling that Ridgecrest Assembly was more than adequate; the West was rather small anyway in constituents, and the outlay of money did not merit such consideration. But the West stood firm in its belief that it would grow and that the need for training would grow larger as time went on.

In addition to this, the committee decided that when a state offered a site for the Convention assembly, it should be a gift! This was quite a setback. In New Mexico there were fewer than 35,000 Baptists in 166 churches. One half of those churches paid their pastors less than one hundred dollars a month. The Baptist headquarters were contained in a makeshift building, although land had been purchased for a new building which was greatly needed. And though the feeling that the cost of the assembly property should be shared was widespread, the committee held firmly to its decision.

When the assembly committee met in St. Louis in 1947, they agreed on a site. However, their report was turned down by the Executive Committee. Part of the assembly committee then withdrew from the larger group and made a recommendation to the Convention for their favorite location. The Executive Committee, however, suggested that the matter be studied for another year, and the Convention accepted this recommendation. This seemed to have eliminated from consideration the property brought before the Convention because of the negative reaction released when proper procedure had been sidestepped.

The committee of nine members continued working throughout the following year, studying sites offered, accessibility, available water, aesthetic beauty, adjacent building and businesses, and other qualifications.

The committee was invited to New Mexico to visit a site in the mountains where a gentleman's agreement had been given Dr. Stagg of its availability to him. Located on the Pecos River, it was near the little town of Pecos; and as the committee gathered there that day, Dr. Stagg found to his great chagrin and heartache that this property had been sold that very hour to the Catholics for a monastery! The price asked was completely out of reason; no notice had been given that another group was considering the property at all. The reaction of the committee was varied, and Dr. Stagg was sadly disappointed. To have the group come from their several states to consider so important a matter and to have it end so abruptly and unexpectedly was, to Harry Stagg, the saddest thing that he could imagine. Any future bid from New Mexico would undoubtedly meet with a negative reaction.

Meanwhile, the state Mission Board of New Mexico waxed and waned between its own emotions concerning whether the need for the assembly to be located in its state superseded its ability to finance such a project. It was overwhelming. For months the huge project had been discussed at the Board meetings. It was difficult to imagine how they could finance the purchase of land without hurting their other local projects. Dr. Stagg, however, remained convinced that a way would be provided.

It came to the attention of Clint Irwin, then pastor of Santa Fe's First Baptist Church, that the Breese Ranch near Glorieta, New Mexico, was up for immediate sale. There were 880 acres of land, and the purchase price was in the amount of $50,000. This fact was brought to the attention of the state Mission Board, but no decision was made. Dr. Stagg then learned that another prospective buyer of the ranch was dealing with Mrs. Breese. With the studied—and rather questioned—approval of the Board, a legal representative offered Mrs. Breese $1,000 to secure a thirty-day option to buy the ranch.

Various churches sent gifts for the project, and the land purchased by the convention for the greatly needed headquarters building for $15,000 was sold for double that amount. This was applied to the note. Santa Fe's First Baptist Church sent the first gift received from a local church, which was in the amount of $1,000. Before the thirty days had passed, the check was given for the full purchase price. And New Mexico Baptists no longer had land for a headquarters building.

Dr. Stagg then notified the assembly committee that a new site had not only been found, but paid for! However, the chairman refused to call a meeting to consider the matter at all. They had come to New Mexico once, he reminded Dr. Stagg, and it had proved to be a wild goose chase. He doubted that New Mexico had anything significant to offer! Besides, the trip was too costly to make again.

The Mission Board was meeting in Portales; and while Dr. Stagg held the telephone, they voted to pay the entire travel cost of the assembly committee to return to New Mexico and study their offer. The chairman still refused. Later, however, several members of the committee did come to Glorieta, although

Dr. Stagg standing on a street in St. Amand, France, during his trip back for revivals with the Foreign Mission Board. His troop was housed in barns on left side of this road, and the hill to the left was site where he went to pray for his mother when he was in WW I. More letters went to her from this village than any other. He went to battle from this place and returned afterwards.

their chairman never did.

At this point a very aggressive promotion began with the help of the Chambers of Commerce of Las Vegas, Santa Fe, and Albuquerque. A very attractive folder was printed concerning the plausibility of a Western Assembly between Santa Fe and Las Vegas, listing the many advantages which they felt were evident. This brochure was then placed in every seat at the Memphis Convention in 1948. There was some criticism to this action; however, it did serve to bring to the attention of the messengers the availability of Glorieta.

The state Mission Board learned in September that the committee's recommendation would be given to the Southern Baptist Convention's Executive Committee in December, 1948. The vote had been 5 to 4 for an Arkansas site. But the board was more committed than ever that the Glorieta property more nearly met the needs for an assembly. Located in the geographic center of the West, easily accessible, with unsurpassed climate and beauty, they decided to hold the offer open to the Southern Baptist Convention until the matter was to be resolved in Oklahoma City in June, 1949.

Philip McGahey, pastor of Albuquerque's First Baptist Church, and C. Vaughan Rock, pastor of the First Southern Baptist Church of Phoenix, Arizona, were on the committee. They were among the four who voted against the Arkansas location. They sought to enlist the other two members to present with them a minority report at the Southern Baptist Convention in Oklahoma City. Even though the other two were opposed to the majority report, they felt that there was nothing in the history of the Convention which would favor the acceptance of a minority report; indeed, it would be better just to forget the Glorieta offer and to go along with the majority. But the two pastors could not forget it so easily. They gathered the needed information, made extensive preparation, and presented their report along with the majority report.

After considerable discussion from the floor of the Convention, it was voted overwhelmingly to authorize a Western Assembly —*and to locate it at Glorieta, New Mexico!*

140

Dr. Duke McCall, then Executive Secretary of the Executive Committee of the Southern Baptist Convention, was seated near Dr. Stagg on the platform. He wrote a note to Dr. Stagg, asking if the New Mexico delegation would oppose a motion to study the qualifications of Glorieta during the following year to be sure that it was an adequate site. Since the committee had not studied it, this would seem wise. The Sunday School Board itself would make the survey. Dr. Stagg replied that not only would such a motion not be opposed; it would be heartily agreed to. No one wanted things right more than Dr. Stagg and the New Mexico Baptists!

After this vote was taken, the Sunday School Board appointed five of its personnel to study the matter throughout the year. They had a long list of qualifications which Dr. Stagg never saw. When they met with Dr. Stagg at a hotel in Santa Fe and pooled their individual lists, it was found that each member had found a complete answer to every question. They gave one hundred percent approval, saying the site was significant in its accessibility, its beauty, and location.

After such overwhelming approval, publication of Glorieta was widespread. But the difficulties were not over! The Sunday School Board insisted that the Baptist Convention of New Mexico make available in clear title to them an additional seven tracts of land adjacent to the Breese Ranch in order to protect the assembly from undesirable developments. When this was discovered, a real-estate agency tied up most of these tracts, and the price was then offered at a terribly inflated cost to New Mexico. After much negotiating, six were secured with much greater cost to Baptists than if they could have dealt with the original owners directly. The seventh tract was owned by a Spanish Catholic in California, and he would not sell it to the real-estate company. However, Judge Sanchez of Santa Fe was a close personal friend of Harry Stagg, and he went to California on behalf of this friendship. He bought the land, returned to New Mexico, and sold it to the Baptist Convention of New Mexico. Another difficult hurdle had been made.

This additional land gave the assembly all property adjoining the Pan-American Highway for about one and three-quarter miles on the south and two miles on the north side. Since this met favorably with the Sunday School Board, Dr. T. L. Holcomb, Executive Secretary of the Board, reported that all the qualifications had been met for development of Glorieta Assembly when the Southern Baptist Convention met in Chicago in 1950.

The Convention adopted the report immediately and instructed the Sunday School Board to proceed with the necessary development of roads, utilities, and buildings; to plan for a full schedule of conferences and other activities similar to those at Ridgecrest; and to open the Glorieta Assembly as soon as possible.

The New Mexico delegation was grateful to God for this decision which they felt was so right and for which they had worked so long and prayed so earnestly. And although the payment for the seven additional tracts of land was forthcoming from the Sunday School Board, the long struggle and setbacks were deep reminders of the emotional cost of such an endeavor. All properties were deeded to the Sunday School Board with the provision that if they ever ceased to be used for the original purpose, the titles would revert to the Baptist Convention of New Mexico.

In addition to the difficulty in securing the additional land, it was discovered that much of it had never been surveyed, platted, or listed in court. Thus there was no actual marketable title. As a result, the Baptist Convention of New Mexico had to have all the community surveyed, a blueprint made, and a plat accepted by the court, plus a suit to establish title agreeable to all in the area. This action involved some people outside the area, and they in turn paid for their part.

Just when Dr. Stagg felt that the situation was under control, the Sunday School Board suggested that since New Mexico Baptists had led in the location of the assembly and the property had been given by them, it was felt that the administration building should be named for New Mexico. However, this would require an outlay of an additional $100,000. The blueprint called for the building eventually to be two and one-half city blocks long and two stories high. When this request was presented to the state Mission Board, the members almost fainted. When they recovered from their shock, they began to rally; they had come this far through an endless, almost impossible task. Surely they could go further in their efforts.

There was no time to falter. They voted to begin a campaign throughout the state for the raising of money for this building. A vigorous campaign was begun; and although the efforts were sometimes discouragingly slow, the goal was ultimately reached. And today the main building at Glorieta carries the name "New Mexico Hall."

One of the most significant involvements with Glorieta in its development and management occurred when Dr. E. A. Herron came as its first manager. He was originally from Louisiana, but grew up in Roswell, New Mexico. He attended Southern Baptist Theological Seminary in Louisville, Kentucky, and served for fourteen years as Sunday School Secretary in New Mexico. For five years he served Alabama Baptists and enjoyed such splendid reputation in the Southern Baptist Convention that his coming to Glorieta for its initial planning and management was most fortunate. He was right at home and enjoyed the confidence of the people whom he served.

One day, along with the committee from the Sunday School Board, Glorieta's architects, and Harry Stagg, they viewed the beautiful property as they sat on a large boulder. Dr. Stagg produced a legal-sized envelope from a coat pocket and drew possible sites for buildings, cottages, maintenance shops, roads, and recreation areas as they visited and planned together. Glorieta was from the beginning planned in most minute detail from a master plan, and it was to take shape much more quickly than one could imagine. Dr. Stagg was invited by the Sunday School Board to sit in on all these planning conferences and was present when bids were opened for most of the major buildings.

In retrospect, Dr. Herron asserts, "God had the Glorieta

grounds ready all along. There is no other place in all those mountains where there is an abundance of water. The Pecos property, originally considered, would not have furnished the half million gallons of water required by the assembly each day. And since in New Mexico no one can dam up any water—even in an arroyo or on private land—the wonderful artesian wells at Glorieta and the draining waters from the mountains have proved to be great blessings." In tribute to his friend Harry Stagg, Dr. Herron says, "From the beginning Dr. Stagg seldom spoke to any group without boosting Glorieta; he has been an untiring booster, counselor, and supporter of the assembly. To him is due most of the credit for the assembly's being located in New Mexico, for its success, and for its everincreasing ministry to our Lord through Southern Baptists."

One marvels at the courage and vision which consumed Dr. Stagg during these long years when faced by such overwhelming odds. But in examining such a stance, one finds the roots of deep conviction which first emerged during the dark days when the young student had to leave college during his severe illness. His dreams of medical mission service had to be channeled into a complete submission to do whatever God wanted him to do. He did not feel a call to be a pastor for life. He was always meant for missions, and his coming to New Mexico was a fulfill-ment of this deep impression. His pastorate at Gallup was a mission pastorate, as difficult at that time as any foreign field. The great mission expansion in the state and his constant urgency and appeal to do more for causes around the world were out-growths of this commitment.

But in the depths of his being, as he wrestled with his severe illness and marveled that God had in no way released him from service, the growing conviction came that if he would be submis-sive and ready, the day would come when he would be a part of something that would be a blessing to the whole Southern Baptist Convention. He had no idea through the years what this might be, but as the vision of Glorieta began to emerge, the strong impression that this was the hour solidified. Through the difficult years, during which he carried on his own work as executive secretary, had major surgery, and endured a lengthy illness—when one setback followed another in the realization of the Glorieta dream—this persuasion held him firmly to the task. It was God's work for him at that time. Surely only a divine sense of purpose would keep one so relentlessly committed to a goal.

As the buildings began to rise, roads were built, beautiful plantings made, and programs began to be offered, it would seem that the troubles were over. However, a day of great alarm was precipitated when the tax assessor of Santa Fe County put all of Glorieta Assembly property on the tax rolls for the sum of ten million dollars! Such a financial crisis would force the closure of the assembly. There was no way it could be paid.

From the beginning until the present time Glorieta Conference Center has paid taxes on all the services rendered—the beauty shop, gift shop, service stations, laundry facilities, and so forth. Taxes had not been assessed for land on which individual cottages were built for properties involved in the training and worship of Glorieta's visitors.

Thus, when all of the assembly was placed on the tax rolls, a great sense of urgency was felt. Consequently, the Sunday School Board brought a lawsuit against the County of Santa Fe and the assessor and officials. When the court convened, Dr. James L. Sullivan, then Executive Secretary of the Sunday School Board, was called as the first witness. The attorneys took adequate time to establish all the official relationships, the legal matters, and the program of Glorieta Assembly. Then Dr. Stagg was called as a witness. All legal papers involved in the purchase of the property were presented to Dr. Stagg for verification and then to the presiding judge. Every legal document carried Dr. Stagg's signature as Executive Secretary of the Baptist convention of New Mexico.

When these papers and relationships of the assembly had been carefully presented, the Santa Fe County attorney asked Dr. Stagg to give a complete statement of the Glorieta story from the very first meeting in Dallas up to the present. This included the purpose and objective of the assembly. The attorney questioned Dr. Stagg in every conceivable manner. After the seemingly endless interrogation, the judge recessed the court for a late lunch period.

It had been arranged for all the Baptist group to have lunch together. Everyone had arrived except their attorney. Much later he arrived, wearing a broad smile. He reported that the county attorney had requested the judge to drop the case and to settle it out of court. The county attorney said, "I cannot get one answer out of Dr. Stagg which I can use on our side of the case. We will simply have to make the necessary adjustments concerning the requests of the assembly and the Sunday School Board."

When the court reconvened at 2:00 P.M., this report was made to the judge. He then requested the attorney representing the Baptist cause to draw up in writing the agreement to submit for the approval of the county attorney and of the court. This was carried out to the agreement of both sides. Land leased for cottages was to be taxed; other grounds were not. And the court so ordered that no subsequent assessor could place the assembly on the tax rolls. It will remain as it is unless the law should change or unless the program and purpose of Glorieta Conference Center changes. Case number 40632 was entered in the books—and the books were closed and shelved.

And so Glorieta stands there today in all its majesty and splendor, a silent testimony to all who pass that Baptists are a vital force, willing to provide in a splendid way for the training and spiritual growth of their constituents.

After the completion of this chapter, Dr. Stagg urged the inclusion of the following as a reaction of one attendant during Glorieta's Pioneer Week. The group worshiped under a huge tent and "camped out" in various kinds of temporary shelters. It rained steadily during the week, making mud puddles everywhere. But nothing seemed to dampen the spirit of the guests. The author's mother, Mrs. L. D. Ball, was there during the week with a group of ladies from First Baptist Church, Lamesa, Texas. So inspired was she by the splendor of all she saw and experienced that she penned these lines, eventually copyrighted, set to music by the author, dedicated to Glorieta Baptist Assembly, and frequently sung there:

Glorieta

Oh, God of all the universe, We want to praise thy name;
For all the beauties of the earth, For oceans, hills, and plains.

Refrain:
For Glorieta, best of all, In thy creative plan;
Thy voice did speak, and it was so—Thy gift from God to man.

Majestic mountains are her walls; Thy handiwork we see;
Her grounds were molded in thy love; We hail thee, King of Kings!

Oh, may her purpose ever be, Thy will to be made known;
To bless the hearts of all mankind, And bring the lost to God!

IX. The Pilot

In the early 1900's when William Stagg was driven home to his Louisiana farm after a revival some distance away, his young son was amazed. That trip normally required a full day by wagon; by car, it was covered in a fraction of the time! Fatigue was lessened, and the day was before him for more productive work. This impressed young Harry tremendously, and he tucked it away in his memory for later reference.

A few years later, the young teenage soldier lay in the cold, muddy trenches of France. Exhausted and war-weary, he often gazed longingly into the clear blue sky as the planes flew overhead in the clean, brilliant heavens. Out of the mire and muck they winged their way, out of the bounds of earth, silhouetted against the sun. Although they were an integral part of the war effort, they were nevertheless lifted above the visible horrors of daily earthbound combat. From the depths of the youthful doughboy's being came the yearning desire, "If only I could fly!"

After feeling almost unbearable pain from having been gassed and from the numerous operations, plus the omnipresent threat of extreme exhaustion, Harry Stagg felt that this was a dream that would never be realized. During the next thirty years of his life he travelled countless miles across the face of the earth, over all kinds of trails, roads, and highways—over endless miles of railroad track. He knew every corner of New Mexico, the fifth largest state in land area in the nation, covering almost 122,000 square miles. When the distance was too great for his schedule, he resorted to commercial flights, trying to adjust himself to their schedules, transfers, delays, and cancellations.

The frequent trips to Nashville had required a week by train; he was grateful that as the old workhorse, the DC-3, came into use, the time required was only one day! (By 1976, the time had been reduced to five and one-half hours with a two-hour stop in Dallas!) He had endured flights endangered by fire, oil leaks, dead engines, and propeller difficulties. But he had also savored many perfect journeys by air. The most breathtaking perhaps was the nonstop flight from Frankfurt, Germany, over the polar ice cap into Chicago. They outflew the sun, leaving Germany one afternoon and arriving at O'Hare International Airport before sundown! He landed in Albuquerque at 8:15 that same day. As they flew over the vast expanses of ice and viewed the ice caps and icebergs, Dr. Stagg marveled at the fantastic beauty of our world and knew that its magnificent grandeur alone would be reason enough to fly.

As Harry Stagg began his last decade of active service to New Mexico Baptists before his retirement, he knew that the work needed all his effort, all of his physical and spiritual powers. Instead of reducing his work load, he needed to increase it! Still plagued with bouts of desperate fatigue, he searched his mind for an answer to the desires he had for increased service as he drove endless miles over difficult highways. Remembering his father, he undoubtedly thought, "When one can spend less time in travel, there is more time left and less fatigue to do one's work." And then came the same haunting urgent yearning born in the trenches of France, "If only I could fly."

One day a friend of Dr. Stagg's, a physician, said, "Harry, you are just beating your life out on the highways. If you could take to the air, your work could be increased remarkably, but you would find it so much easier, so much quicker." The doctor, himself a pilot, counseled with him many times about the wisdom of somehow acquiring a small aircraft to enlarge his work and conserve his physical energies. Harry Stagg, already past his middle fifties, realized that most pilots were thinking of retiring at that age, not learning to fly! He was quickly reassured that he could easily learn to pilot a plane and that his other physical disabilities were no more a hindrance to flying than driving a car.

Tantalized by these continuing suggestions, the busy minister decided to conduct his own feasibility study as to the practicality of using a plane in his work. He discovered that many ranchers throughout the state used planes extensively. Many owned their own planes and had built private landing strips. They maintained radio contact with other aircraft, often answering questions as to weather conditions in their area. They also shared landing strips and would frequently touch down long enough for a little visit and refreshment. He found that most of the oil company executives used airplanes almost exclusively. The large business companies conserved the energies and time of their executives by the use of private aircraft.

In connection with this research, Dr. Stagg was taken on numerous demonstration flights by various agencies who dealt in aircraft sales. The demonstrators took him to various appointments throughout the state—the first of which was to Gallup. En route to his former hometown, they passed near the almost perfectly formed volcanic crater where many of the Staggs' friends had picnicked, some venturing even to the basin of the crater. Harry expressed a desire to see it more closely— whereupon the pilot said, "You have the controls. Go where you like!" With a feather touch on the wheel, Dr. Stagg felt the complete response of the plane as seconds later they were directly over the crater which he had passed many different times over the years, but only now felt he was really seeing.

These flights, combined with what Dr. Stagg had already learned and the needs he felt were so pressing, fully convinced him of the practicability, safety, and economy of the use of an airplane for Baptist work in New Mexico. At that time, no other state convention, to Dr. Stagg's knowledge, owned the title to and operated its own plane. But, believing in the approach so strongly, he set about to study the next requirement: financing.

That fall, as he went to the various annual associational meetings throughout the state, Dr. Stagg mentioned his growing belief of the value of air travel for the staff. After his message in Eunice, one of the senior Baptist laymen, "Uncle" Mark Owen, approached him and discussed that subject more fully. When the state convention met the following month in Albuquerque, Dr. Stagg determined to pursue the matter of Mr. Owen's interest in a plane for the state. After one of the sessions, Dr. Stagg asked him for an appointment. Smiling, and with a twinkle in his eyes, Mr. Owen said, "You don't need an appointment with me. I know what you want, and I have already decided what I am going to do about it. If you want to pursue this program, I will send you a check for $5,000."

This was a tremendous boost to Harry Stagg's dream and purpose for his third decade as executive secretary. He presented his findings to the state Mission Board for discussion and received their affirmative vote to proceed with the additional financing and purchase of a small plane. It would be owned and officially operated by the Baptist Convention of New Mexico.

After the exhaustive investigation and demonstrations made, Dr. Stagg settled on a plane. It was available in February, 1957. The very first trip made in the new plane was to Farmington on Valentine's Day. The volunteer pilot was a woman who later flew in the Powderpuff Derby. (Her doctor-husband was the friend who urged Dr. Stagg to consider flying.) This official flight also included a delivery from the Baptist Book Store to the church they were scheduled to meet with.

Since Dr. Stagg could spare a little time during his days in Albuquerque, he secured the services of top flight instructors and began lessons himself. Most of his training was in cross-country, going to appointments. Usually the instructors went to the services with the preacher and listened to him speak. It was a particular thrill that the very first instructor was converted and baptized as a result of his lessons with the busy minister.

Looking back over his eventful life, Dr. Stagg declares that May 2, 1957, would undoubtedly go down as one of the most exciting days he ever experienced. "This was the day," he states almost twenty years later, "when I realized I was soaring in an airplane high in yonder blue over the west mesa at Albuquerque—my first solo flight! I know of no words to adequately express this experience. I have never read of an experience that could completely describe it."

As he flew alone for the first time, he did some of the most earnest praying of his lifetime. He realized that it was up to him to control the plane and to put it safely back on the runway at the end of the flight. He talked to God about the use of the plane in the mission work of the state and prayed that it would be used in a beneficial way to the conclusion of his ministry. From the first, it was dedicated to God and used for his glory.

It was a good "touch and go." After the flight, the plane was put down on the runway, and Harry emerged to the congratulations of his faithful instructor. This was a never-to-be-forgotten day, the culmination of months of investigation, experimentation, study, and serious consideration of the use of the airplane in the work of the convention.

Mrs. Stagg and their grandson, Jim Cantrell, served as the first passengers for the new pilot. Always supportive in whatever her husband did, Alma Stagg took sufficient training that she herself was fully qualified to fly the plane, to take off and land, to navigate anywhere. She could communicate over the radio and check the weather and air traffic controls. One of Dr. Stagg's cardinal beliefs about flying is that there should always be someone besides the pilot on board who is qualified to take over the controls in case of an emergency. This belief put into practice, plus the other careful rules of safety which he followed, were undoubtedly the reasons he chalked up so many thousands of safe miles in the air.

Because of Mrs. Stagg's petite stature, she could not reach the rudder pedals on the aircraft. This deterred her not a whit. They simply took an old pair of shoes to the shoe shop and had an extension built up on the back of the heels so she could be as effective as she needed to be. These shoes, of course, were kept in the plane and were waiting whenever she required them for flying.

Added to this help from his wife, Harry learned everything

Dr. and Mrs. Harry P. Stagg
Golden Wedding Anniversary

he could about the machine he was flying. Whenever he taxied into a hangar and requested two or three adjustments to be made by the mechanic, they knew that he understood his business. Anyone who thought he was just a "novice out for a Sunday ride" quickly found that the reverse was true. One of his pilot friends said of him, "He knows every screw in that plane, every adjustment needed—possibly more than some of the mechanics."

And so the staff at the Baptist headquarters "took to the air." Several could fly at once, and the shared expense seemed to check out admirably with previous travel allotments. Indeed, in the 1963 convention annual the report stated that during the last five years, of the 600,000 passenger miles travelled by the staff, the travel budget had been maintained. The farthest point in the state could be reached in ninety minutes, and the four-hour car trip to Roswell could be made in fifty minutes by plane. Along with time and energy conserved, the staff found that they could make more appointments and get back into Albuquerque for office work less fatigued. Because they did not have to go through commercial scheduling and baggage checks, other valuable time and effort was conserved.

At the time of the beginning of the use of the aircraft, there were sixty-eight approved airstrips in New Mexico. Only ten or twelve New Mexico cities at that time were served by commercial planes. There was no electronic navigation equipment available at that time—only a north-south, east-west radio beam which used the old "beep beep" method, but it was followed gratefully. Rather rapidly, however, the electronic equipment became available with the VOR service. And on the average, those flying were able to cut travel time to one-fourth that which had been required by car. The car mileage allowance was used on the same basis for the plane; and the expenses, as stated, paralleled closely.

They quickly found that New Mexico was one of the best-adapted states in the Union for air service. The long distances of open country and the topography of the terrain made it possible for them to fly to any part of the state without having

154

to go over the many high mountain ridges. Because the staff traveled at the invitation of the churches or associations to which they went, there were always local people who were most gracious to meet their plane and give them car transportation the short distance to the appointment. These personal encounters were an unexpected benefit.

Landing strips were enough in abundance that there was no difficulty in getting to their appointments. But the accommodations of the strips differed widely! The landing on a little dirt strip on the Navajo Reservation at Tinian was a case in point. Before the Baptist delegation could land, someone on the ground had to get the grazing sheep out of the way! At Carrizozo, on the anniversary of the founding of the church, one of the military personnel from White Sands Proving Grounds had made the delicious birthday cake; and nearby, landing in a cow pasture, were the guests of the day!

One of the most spectacular airports in the state is located at Los Alamos. For many years that city was closed to the general public, and the airport provided only for official transportation and certain local residents. Happily, a permit to land was extended the Baptist Convention of New Mexico, so air transportation to that city was also available. The airstrip in Los Alamos has only one runway. Landings are made toward the mountain, while takeoffs are made toward the valley. Extreme caution must be taken because of shifting air currents and the sheer cliffs.

When a group went to Shiprock for a conference with the Indian constituency there, they landed on a little dirt strip. After takeoff they circled the famous historical marker, the Shiprock itself, rising out of the vast expanse of desert land, memorable and hallowed to the Indians as a sacred ship from the sky.

On the trips to Nashville or flights to the Southern Baptist Conventions, the accommodations were much different. Perhaps the most plush, red-carpet treatment of all was at Dulles International Airport in Washington, D.C. There were scores of acres of concrete and planes of all kinds from countries around the world. They were accorded every courtesy an aircraft could possibly receive as air traffic control placed them in sequence for landing along with the largest planes, and then radioed the place for reporting. The fixed-base operators were most cordial and helpful, even lending a car for the group to use to ride to the main terminal for dinner.

The use of the plane opened new doors of opportunity and friendship never before available or accessible. A professional painter was employed to paint two concentric circles on either side of the brown plane. The words "Baptist Convention of New Mexico" were printed along the outside rim of the larger circle, and "Albuquerque" was printed across the center. Numerous questions about the words were raised wherever they landed, and an avenue for Christian witness was opened. It was excellent advertising. Indeed, the whole program of flight gave the convention an aura of esteem and recognition not previously enjoyed. As Dr. Stagg spoke on behalf of Baptists before colleges and universities, at high school commencements, at Chambers of Commerce, and at various Rotary clubs, these groups took note of the businesslike manner and wide involvement of the Baptist convention of the state.

The Royal Ambassadors of the Southern Baptist Convention engaged in a contest to name the plane. From everywhere came suggestions. At last, as the names were carefully sifted through, one was chosen. It was "Amigo"—"Friend." By having this one Spanish word printed on either side of the plane near the cowling, immediate recognition was given to the multicultural population of New Mexico.

And in Nashville, the newspapers heralded the new approach to transporting Baptists for Convention-wide meetings. Complete with pictures, the story written was engaging, indeed.

Perhaps the busiest day the active executive had included six appointments, ranging from Farmington in the northwest to Roswell and Clovis in the southeastern part of the state—and then the return home. Only one of these meetings would have been possible by car. Dr. Stagg, looking back, continues to feel that the use of the plane was one of the most valuable investments

156

made by Baptists of the state. It more than doubled his ministry, and the staff used it widely as well. He felt that this was a definite answer to special prayer: God was kind and gracious. His spiritual sights were lifted; his ambition and insights seemed to be multiplied as never before as he entered his last years of active ministry.

He continues to thank God that he was able to take wings and soar above the heavens, far above the contamination of things below. In those days he suffered considerably from hay fever; driving across the arid state caused him extreme difficulty. However, as he flew above the dust and pollen he experienced great relief. This was a spiritual lesson to him as he recognized that we get contaminated with all kinds of "pollen" that cut our usefulness as Christians and reduce our spiritual health. When that happens, he mused, we need to rise into the presence of God and be freed of these difficulties.

Many necessary trips were made in the plane to Nashville. It was usually found that one fuel stop was adequate en route. To their amazement, the staff discovered that they often flew past a DC-3 with considerable ease. The fastest trip was undoubtedly from Albuquerque to Oklahoma City when the average speed was 204 m.p.h. And the slowest had to be a return trip from Nashville via Lubbock, Texas. Out of Lubbock they flew into a tremendous head wind. They teased later that it required twenty minutes just to cross the narrow Pecos River! Appalled by their slow speed, they decided to land at the abandoned military airport at Fort Sumner. The next morning, on a clear day, they flew back into Albuquerque.

On a flight from Amarillo, considerable turbulence was experienced before they reached Tucumcari. Horace Burns, then editor of the *Baptist New Mexican,* remarked later that he had rededicated his life three times during that short distance! After a radio survey was made, it was decided to land for the night in Tucumcari rather than to risk the trip into home base. When problems occurred en route from Washington, D.C., they settled down in Virginia for the night and awoke to a beautiful new day, much better suited for flying. On a return trip from Hobbs, and ten minutes out of Roswell, Dr. Stagg discovered that the carburetor's de-icing control had broken. The butterfly valve could thus flip either way; it could be closed for prevention of icing or opened where there was no control or protection at all. It was unthinkable that he could continue toward home and fly over the Sandias. He turned back to Roswell, had the repairs made, and then flew home safely.

While the engine was revving up for takeoff in Albuquerque one cold morning, the carburetor flooded and caught fire from a back fire. The attendant quickly extinguished the flame with little damage except for their cancelled flight until they were cleared by a mechanic.

These mishaps, all minor, were about the only delays experienced during the convention's thirteen-year ownership of the planes. When weighed against the expanded ministry possible, they are negligible indeed. After four years, the convention bought a new, larger plane and used the smaller one as a trade, receiving more for it than it had cost new. Many people told Dr. Stagg that the convention owned the best-equipped private plane in the Southwest. His firm belief in proper maintenance no doubt contributed to the total picture of flight safety.

When the Southern Baptist Convention met in Atlantic City, Dr. Stagg was invited by Dr. Loyd Corder of the Home Mission Board to accompany him on an exploratory trip to New York. They flew up the coast from Washington, D.C. and along the shore passing New York City and Long Island. They surveyed this expanse of land for the purpose of extending Baptist work in that area. It was a beautifully clear day and a fantastic sight. Everything was plainly visible, even the palisades up the Hudson River. The famous Riverside Church rose heavenward in the brilliant day, and the Statue of Liberty stood as a sentinel in the harbor. The next day they left Atlantic City and flew to Atlanta, their geographic survey completed.

One of the most amazing things about the flying program, Dr. Stagg believes, was the way in which God provided pilot assistants. Bill Manus, an air traffic controller, was a dedicated Baptist and an Albuquerque resident. Because of his heavy responsibilities and the pressure under which he worked, Mr. Manus had considerable time free. Having been a military pilot during the war, he was eager to keep up with his flying. He piloted the plane or assisted with it for many years. His skill, ability, and knowledge provided expert protection and leadership. Later he wanted to give up his regular job and take one with the FAA instrument plane as pilot. When he filed an application for this position, they required a certain amount of active flying during the previous twelve-month period. To his delight, the time spent flying the convention's plane was accepted one hundred percent.

Later Joe Carl Johnson was on the staff of the state convention. An experienced pilot, he was invaluable for a number of years in this area. When his appointments coincided with Dr. Stagg's or were en route to his, they could share the piloting duties. And pilot Leo Sullivan came to the fore when Mr. Johnson left for service in Panama and then the Home Mission Board, where he continues to serve. Mr. Sullivan came as pastor of Bethel Baptist Church in Albuquerque and gave valuable service in the flying program.

Phil Card has been associated with the Colorado Baptist Convention for many years. He had previously been associated with the Air Force and continued his status as a reserve pilot and instructor. Because he attended many of the same Southern Baptist Convention meetings as the New Mexico staff, he often accompanied them. Dr. Stagg logged many hours under his expert instruction, profited from his experience, and enjoyed wonderful Christian fellowship with him. As a special favor, he accompanied Dr. Stagg to Nashville on the latter's last trip before his retirement.

"It is amazing," Harry Stagg recalls, "how God provided the very best in knowledge, experience, and ability." As he considers the advisability of such transportation in today's world, he fully realizes that many of the provisions previously available would be utterly impossible now. The startling increase in the cost of aircraft, the many government regulations imposed because of present-day society, the increase of aircraft in flight, the tremendous increase in the cost of fuel and maintenance—all are negative factors. "But," he insists, "much of the difficulty of our society today can be traced to a breakdown in the moral and spiritual fiber of our nation and the world. The very purpose for which we purchased the airplane—to more effectively preach the gospel of Christ and the individual redemption through faith in him—is more needed today than ever before in the history of the world."

Today as Dr. Stagg takes out his old, "beat-up" flight case, his mind is flooded with wonderful memories. Tracing with a finger his name etched on the brown leather, he opens it to days of the past. His charts and the old Air Force computer used before the electronic navigation came into service are there. The real story, however, is in the well-used log book, with its list of instructors and the air base operators who signed his log on his cross-country flights. Page after page of neat entries are there, recording necessary information of flights, but conjuring up complete stories of what really happened on each trip. Memories of the pastors and church leaders, of important events which transpired and those who accompanied him—all are there, reminding him of blessed days of the past.

Although there may be many facets to a life, there should be no distinction with the Christian between the sacred and the mundane. All of life should be dedicated, set apart, for God's service. And, consistent with this tenet throughout Dr. Stagg's life, he learned not only the mechanics of flying. Superimposed on these facts were spiritual truths, allegorical to the nuts and bolts of piloting an aircraft.

Just after his first formal flying lesson was concluded, Dr. Stagg's instructor handed him a large amount of printed material to read. At their next encounter, his teacher asked if everything was clear. "Yes," replied the minister, "except I have wondered about a typographical error throughout the books—shouldn't 'altitude' be used instead of 'attitude' in these pages?" The pilot-teacher laughed and said, "That is one of the greatest lessons you can learn in flying. The most important word to remember at all times is not 'altitude' but 'attitude.' " Soon Dr. Stagg found that this meant the position of the airplane in relationship to heaven and earth. In a plain, practical way, it means whether the aircraft is going up or down or is level between earth and heaven. And surely, for a Christian, the proper attitude, the proper relationship between heaven and earth must be maintained for abundant living.

Another lesson Dr. Stagg learned was that constant maintenance is the greatest safety factor in flying an airplane. A plane cannot run smoothly unless all its parts are in good working condition. He learned that one must follow the book; to take off on one's own intuition only leads to disaster. A flight plan must be filed; there should be a purpose, a master design. One should not leave the ground without a copilot, and he should never hesitate to turn around and go back or to alter a plan if things do not go as expected. He says that the 180-degree turn is the greatest safety device ever invented. Adequate insurance was also carried in the event that unexpected events occurred.

He found that if a plane goes down faster than its *maximum* performance speed, it will probably fall apart before it crashes. If it tries to climb faster than its limitations, it will stall and fall like a chunk of wood. Every plane has its limitations of range and service. Every pilot has his range of abilities and service. No pilot who ever lived can fly a plane beyond its potential; no plane can attain its highest performance without a proper pilot applying his maximum skills. And in our own lives, we must maintain an average of performance suitable to our abilities.

Every plane, he discovered, has its *minimum* flying speed; and this speed must be maintained or the plane will crash. The weight and balance are of great importance. If an engine was lost, the weight and balance must be such that the nose of the plane would automatically drop. Control of the craft would thus be possible as the flying speed could be maintained in a glide. He also learned that *everything* can fall by gravity. He saw that in every increase of altitude, there is a decrease in available power, and that it takes additional power to achieve an increase in altitude *unless the plane is supercharged by a costly device!*

Each of these lessons, so pragmatic and basic, was lifted into the spiritual realm and hallowed as the minister-pilot meditated on its truth as he logged almost half a million miles for the cause of Baptist work in New Mexico.

In the years of his piloting aircraft, Dr. Stagg experienced many wonderful feelings of closeness to God, of being lifted out of the earth's miasma temporarily—but returning quickly to become a part, hopefully, of the solution. These emotions are entirely different from anything experienced on the surface of the earth. Our returning astronauts have shared with us the lofty thoughts and emotions toward God which they experienced while visiting the moon or orbiting the earth. John Gillespie Magee, Jr., a young pilot killed early in World War II, attempted to express in his poem "High Flight" the emotions of countless air travelers as they have soared above the stringent bounds of earth. Carol Stagg Tope reprinted and framed the poem, and it now hangs in her parents' home:

> Oh! I have slipped the surly bonds of Earth,
> And danced the skies on laughter-silvered wings;
> Sunward I've climbed, and joined the tumbling mirth
> Of sun-split clouds—and done a hundred things
> You have not dreamed of—wheeled and soared and swung
> High in the sunlit silence. Hov'ring there,
> I've chased the shouting wind along, and flung
> My eager craft through footless halls of air.
>
> Up, up the long, delirious, burning blue
> I've topped the wind-swept heights with easy grace,
> Where never lark, or even eagle flew—
> And, while with silent, lifting mind I've trod
> The high untrespassed sanctity of space,
> Put out my hand, and touched the face of God.[1]

[1] From *Poems for the Great Days,* compiled by Thomas Curtis Clark and Robert Earle Clark. © Copyright by Abingdon-Cokesbury Press (Nashville, 1948), p. 96. Used by permission of Abingdon Press.

X. The Preacher

There was an air of excitement at Gallup that Armistice Day. A large crowd of people had gathered from miles around to hear a famous United States senator speak. The porch of the new post office would serve as the platform. The meeting had begun when suddenly the plea came over the public address system that if Rev. Harry Stagg were in the audience, his presence was immediately requested on the platform. The preacher was indeed present, and until that moment had been enjoying himself immensely. He made his way to the stage quickly and discovered to his horror that the senator would not be able to be present because of travel complications—and would he please consent to make the address instead! He made the speech.

Some years later in Albuquerque, the Baptist Student Center was to be dedicated at the University of New Mexico. It was an auspicious occasion. The state convention was in session at the time, and in addition to dignitaries from all over New Mexico and Baptist leaders from the Southern Baptist Convention headquarters, the Governor and his staff were in attendance, as well as the president of the university and many of his faculty. There was an overflow attendance. The speaker was an official from the Sunday School Board. But while the program marched forward and no speaker appeared in view, the situation began to get a little tense.

About five minutes before time for the address to be given, someone whispered to Dr. Stagg, who was sitting on the stage, that the speaker's plane was down in Tucumcari and he could not possibly get to Albuquerque! There was nothing to do, he said, but for Dr. Stagg to speak. He had the length of one verse of song to get his thoughts together, and address the group he did in a very appropriate manner. When asked what he did under these circumstances, he, replied, "I turned white."

Being able to speak extemporaneously and inspirationally at the same time have always been two of his wonderful talents. He never wrote his sermons down, but read from many sources and always said something relevant, informative, interesting, and challenging. His messages were remembered, and people, years after hearing him, have commented on the impact of a particular message to their lives. Often, when he felt he had the message in mind which he would deliver, he would alter it partially or completely in order to speak to an urgent need which had come to his attention during the service. His messages were always fresh and meaningful as a result. His wife gently teases him today as she recalls the deacon who used to pray for him before he spoke in Gallup: "And dear Lord, please bless our pastor as he *prepares* to preach!"

Once he addressed the student body at Louisiana College and used a great deal of information concerning Mesa Verde National Park in Colorado. He had never visited the park, although he had read extensively about it. When the family returned to New Mexico, they went by Colorado to check out the truth of what had been read in books and reported to the college students against what was actually there. It all checked out.

He was introduced as guest speaker for a men's service club in Abilene, Texas, and arose to face his audience. He launched out in Cajun, a very-difficult-to-understand mixture of French and English. His listeners began to smile and chuckle, whereupon he stopped, looked dismayed and embarrassed, and explained that he had very little education and was simply doing the best he could. "Not everybody," he continued, "could live in a city with 'tre university.' " The members of the club then looked chagrined and began to listen attentively as they strained to understand his diction. Suddenly Dr. Stagg himself could restrain no longer and burst into laughter. The club joined in, realizing that he had really had the last laugh. He then brought a serious, challenging address. Afterward a businessman asked him to reproduce the identical speech—from Cajun start to American English finish (with heavy southern flavor)—for his employees. Harry deeply appreciated the invitation, but his schedule would not permit this addition.

While Harry Stagg was pastor in Gallup, Dr. Rock had given him a standing invitation to address the First Southern Baptist Church in Phoenix on each New Year's Day. For thirteen consecutive years he found this to be a meaningful experience for him as well as the church. When he became executive secretary for New Mexico Baptists, however, he could no longer give that time, although he treasured the memory of his association with that fine church.

One of his most memorable experiences during the Gallup years was speaking for the Ganado Presbyterian Mission. This was a full mission station with a hospital, a church, a school, and nurses' training provided. When the building for the nurses was completed, Harry Stagg preached the dedicatory sermon and later spoke to one of their graduating classes. There was also a five-day Chautauqua held where about six hundred Navajo Indians were in attendance. Dr. Stagg had the rare privilege of speaking to them on a daily basis, under a big circus tent.

When the first Royal Ambassador National Conference was held in Fort Worth, Texas, he was guest speaker. Near Fort Worth, on a large ranch, a full-scale rodeo was held to entertain the boys. Dr. Stagg, as cowboy chaplain for the occasion, rode the horse which belonged to the rodeo manager. Dressed in full western regalia which included the big white cowboy hat, he had two huge six-shooters strapped to his waist with a wide, engraved leather belt. He wore "high-powered" cowboy boots. The horse, well trained for his responsibilities, knew exactly what to do; the rider only had to stay on him! They made the grand parade and the circles, next going to the campfire in the center of the arena. The preacher then dismounted and conducted a religious service for those who were gathered around.

There are probably few Baptist pulpits in the state where Dr. Stagg has not stood many times. In addition, he has addressed about every university and college in the state and many high school baccalaureates. He gave the first commencement address at Grand Canyon College in Phoenix, Arizona, and was also the first commencement speaker for Golden Gate Seminary. He has been called upon to address civic groups and Chambers of Commerce as well as to speak to denominational meetings in surrounding states. He has preached in Copenhagen, Denmark, where he brought greetings from Townley Lord, then President of the Baptist World Alliance, whom Dr. Stagg had just visited in London. He has preached in Nazareth and Cana, in Frankfurt, Germany, and in other places too numerous to mention.

Perhaps one of the many highlights of his preaching ministry came during the annual revival at Hardin-Simmons University in Abilene, Texas. Returning veterans from World War II were picking up their educations and entering civilian life once more. It was the writer's privilege to be a part of that endeavor and to see countless lives committed to Christ during that unforgettable week. Years later, those who have remained closely associated with the university look upon that week as a spiritual high-water mark. Numerous youth were subsequently involved in Baptist work in New Mexico as a direct result of that week: Christine Waddill, Gerald Palmer, Bernard Dougharty, and Bill Shearin, to name a few.

The only New Mexico Baptist ever tapped to preach the annual sermon for a Southern Baptist Convention has been Harry P. Stagg. It was a signal honor to him as well as to the state he served.

While conducting a revival for the Gambrell Street Baptist Church in Fort Worth, just across the way from Southwestern Baptist Theological Seminary, he had opportunity to speak in chapel for that school and then to speak to the church history classes concerning the work in New Mexico. Wherever he found himself, his heart and thoughts were always with his beloved adopted state.

A number of times during his long ministry, Dr. Stagg used the illustration concerning the training of the oxen during his boyhood years. He smiles when he recalls preaching it during

Music Week at Glorieta, but remembers that the musicians could identify with it. When asked to relate it once more, he became very serious and, to an appreciative audience of one, repeated the valuable lessons he had learned from those animals on his father's farm.

The oxen must be completely obedient and submissive to their trainer. When they are called to the yoke they are completely committed to the driver's will until he releases them. No one ox can pull independently as horses can; they must pull together. They can, however, equalize the burden if one is *able* to pull a little more.

When you want to change directions, you speak to the proper one, and he speeds up for the pivot as the other holds his pace. The front yoke is trained to select the best trail.

If they don't obey, there is a way to correct them. The ox whip carries a grass cracker (plaited smaller than a whip), and its main purpose is to make noise. When the driver pops it, the oxen usually listen. If this does not succeed after about three attempts, the whip is allowed to sting the ox in a vulnerable spot (this is used only as a last resort by a good trainer).

When the team gets stuck, they can pull out *if they pull together*. They cannot pull out if they continue to go the same way as they did when they became stuck. There is one exception; if the yoke itself is used as a lever while one of the oxen stands stolidly and the other moves with the yoke, the impasse may be solved.

The examples for the Christian in his relationship to God and the need for cooperation with others are obvious and meaningful.

Almost from the beginning of Harry Stagg's arrival in the state, the *New Mexico Baptist Annuals* carry his name as he was elected to various positions or spoke in one of the conventions. Beginning as pastor of the smallest church in the state (Gallup had only five members in 1925), he nevertheless had the needs of the world on his heart. When the convention met in Las Cruces in 1933 his text was taken from Deuteronomy 6:23: "And he brought us out from thence, that he might bring us in, to give us the land which he sware unto our fathers." Even in the midst of the great depression, he urged a positive, expansive approach to evangelizing his adopted state.

After Dr. Stagg became executive secretary-treasurer for the state he spoke to the conventions on an annual basis. In almost every instance he commended the group to whom he was speaking for the excellent work done during the preceding year and then challenged them to do more for God's glory during the next twelve months. No matter what his theme, this urgency to do more was present. And for thirty years he held this divine imperative aloft. One need only to examine the records to find the results.

In 1946, when he had been executive secretary for nine years, he had exceeded in time the service of any former executive. And his Southern voice rang out as clear and as fresh as before as he preached on the subject "Hills to Climb." In 1951 at the annual convention in Clovis he spoke on stewardship and what could be accomplished if all Baptists tithed. The next year as he addressed the WMU about "Exalting Christ in New Mexico," he stated that the only way this could be accomplished was on a worldwide basis. "New Mexico is blessed with a different atmosphere—physical, social, spiritual," he stated. "Our pastors should be sent to participate in worldwide evangelistic campaigns in order for us to wield an international influence." The very dramatic culture in which New Mexicans lived, therefore, could be used for God's glory.

Two years later in Roswell he declared: "We need to expand, extend, enlarge, step up, and speed up every activity and agency of our state mission program." And he continued in the same vein when he addressed the men: "The greatest challenge in the Christian world lies with the work and program of the Southern Baptist Convention. We are missing the mark in national and international leadership, and it is high time someone did something about it."

In 1960 he called for the strengthening of the Cooperative Program, to stop "playing Baptists" as we entered our fiftieth year. To the Woman's Missionary Union Convention he read the account in Luke 14:18 where excuses were made to avoid doing the Lord's bidding because one had bought a field and

168

had to see it, and another had bought five yoke of oxen and needed to prove them. In his message, Dr. Stagg deplored the trend of United States citizens to declare bankruptcy because "I have bought." He stated that much of Baptist work had to be revised downward because inflation had nullified much of our giving; our stewardship simply had not kept up with the increase in salaries and the cost of living. "But," he continued, "the things of the world are still going upward because 'we have bought' the things that we *most* desire and have left out the work of the Lord. Evangelical work has leveled off the last year; the liquor and tobacco industries have not." And he concluded forcefully, "There is no tomorrow for us. If the lost are to be won, they must be won today."

In 1963 Dr. Stagg made a sentimental journey back to Europe, where he had fought so valiantly during World War I. The purpose was not purely emotional, however; his major concern dealt with the evangelistic campaign he participated in under the direction of the Foreign Mission Board. After reminiscing about some of his days on the battlefields of France forty-five years before, he stated to the convention that November:

I came back with a deeper sense of responsibility than ever before. If we just had the same spirit of sacrifice that those soldiers had, what we could do for Christ! This convention is turning the tide. You watch the ocean. The tide eases out, and after a while it comes back. We have been on dead center now for about four years, but this convention is the turn, and the tide has started up. I challenge you tonight—let's do something about this; let's do it immediately and accomplish the thing that God wants us to do in this state.

When the Baptists converged on Hobbs for the 1965 annual convention, Harry Stagg spoke on the subject "The Heart of Our State Program—Proclaiming Christ" and stated that if we believe in miracles, now is a good time to produce one. He referred to the union of many churches with the Roman Catholic Church and noted that there "are one hundred and fifteen programs through which churches can get tax money from the government. Catholics and Communists are on a crash program to see who can get our nation first."

He then told of the spectacular and rapid changes in government and society in our world and how the Ecumenical Council had proclaimed religious liberty for its constituents. He scoffed at this being thought of as a new philosophy, declaring that Baptists have done this—have fought and died for this—throughout our history. He further mentioned that he had participated in more dedication services for new church buildings in 1965 than ever before, and he earnestly prayed that it means that there would be a strengthening of the work in these churches. And when he stood before the WMU convention later, he said humbly and from the heart: "All that I am is because of New Mexico Baptists."

As a result of the strong stand he took concerning federal funding of religious organizations, the convention made the following resolution:

Resolved: That we reaffirm our belief in freedom of religion and the separation of church and state, that we deplore the use of millions of dollars of federal funds to support religious institutions, that we strongly urge our Baptist colleges, universities and other institutions to refrain from taking government financial aid. Be it resolved that we express by this resolution, and with standing ovation, the courageous stand of our Executive Secretary, Dr. Harry P. Stagg, for his strong contention of religious freedom and the fundamentals of our historic faith. We stand alongside you, Dr. Stagg, because we know by your clear voice that you are standing for truth and righteousness. We stand alongside you, our brother, because we know you stand for the exalting of our Lord and Savior Jesus Christ.

The message to the 1966 convention would have normally been the last message as executive secretary because Dr. Stagg had reached—indeed, he had passed—retirement age. The state Mission Board asked him to stay one more year, and he considered that request one of the greatest compliments of his entire lifetime. The same sense of world awareness, of duty to God and pride in his state, came through as clearly as it had twenty-nine years earlier when he had stood before them for the first time as their leader. He described the terrain of the United

States, pointing out that New Mexico was blessed with beautiful valleys, majestic mountains, great rivers—the Pecos, the Canadian, the historic Rio Grande, and the San Juan—a variety of climate and scenery of unsurpassing beauty for which we should thank God. He spoke of the abundance of products such as oil, uranium, gas, potash, coal, copper, cotton, cattle, beans, peanuts, and apples.

He then described the various projects of the federal government which contribute to our economy, such as the nuclear research projects, the scientific laboratories, and missile ranges. With people coming into the state to work in these areas, to participate in the military, and to become associated with the universities, "we have the world right at our doorstep in regard to opportunity and service," he said. "But," he warned, "one fourth of the Baptists in the state are keeping up with the expenses of the work. And in the twenty-nine years that I have served as your executive secretary, my hair has turned from black to silver—but that is the only thing around that has turned to silver!"

When Harry Stagg entered Hoffmantown Baptist Church in Albuquerque on November 14, 1967, it was the forty-third consecutive convention he had attended in New Mexico. It was his last as executive secretary and was never to be forgotten by him and Mrs. Stagg. As he was presented to the Brotherhood Convention, the presiding officer announced him as "Mr. Baptist of New Mexico, the man of the hour, man of the day, man of the month, man of the year, and man of our generation in New Mexico." And when he was given opportunity to respond, he did not look back toward what he had seen accomplished in New Mexico, but held aloft once more the golden torch of opportunity. One can feel the yearning in his heart as he appealed to them one last time:

Baptists should and must stand fast to what the Bible teaches about the birth of Jesus Christ and baptism by immersion . . . We as Southern Baptists should not accept funds from the government for our schools; however, it seems that within the next few years the government will force schools to accept funds or they will have to close their doors

. . . Our mission challenge is to touch the lives of those who never attend church, never give anything to mission causes, and we must never be willing to write them off as a lost cause . . . There is a revolution taking place in our land—in our Indian reservations and among our Spanish-speaking friends . . . The recreational areas of our state present a tremendous challenge to our mission field . . . We are challenged with the need to reach the young people on our campuses, our colleges, and high schools . . . Let us stay true to the Word and let God take care of the rest.

Throughout his ministry, there were two major themes to which Dr. Stagg addressed himself. Wherever he spoke, this philosophy broke through either directly or indirectly. The first concerned his strong belief in the church. "It is the only plan the Lord made to carry on the work from his ascension to his second coming," he declares. And he held forth the truth that the church is the only organization, the only institution; it is the church or nothing. All the added programs and activities may help the church, but they can never take the place it has to preach the gospel to every creature in all the world or to teach them to observe the truth.

If the church does not carry out its responsibility, these things left to it will not be done. "Every movement in the world has come about to lead away from this main line of the church, but it cannot be done," he continues. And he emphasizes that the most important commitment a Christian can ever make is to be made through the church as a local organization. And then churches have opportunity to cooperate in unlimited fashion. Everything he tried to do included the strengthening of the local body of Christians.

The other major emphasis involved Dr. Stagg's strong stand concerning the separation of church and state—or the freedom of political government and the freedom of the religious convictions. There is no way one can control the other without disastrous results. Coming from a stronghold of Catholicism in Louisiana to a state where the Roman Church had been dominant for centuries, he knew firsthand the difficulties such involvements could cause and stood firm in this important issue.

XI. The Rotarian

In the winter of 1926-27, Dr. Stagg was invited to become a member of the Rotary Club in Gallup. Although he was only twenty-eight years old, and that international organization is composed largely of more mature and proven men in their fields, his name was submitted and approved for membership. The principles of the club and the purpose for the meetings were such that the greatly appreciated invitation was accepted. This was eventually to serve as a "window to the world" for Harry Stagg as he, on a weekly basis, came into contact with world leaders, specialists in the scientific area and office holders in government. He has attended meetings around the world during his travels and is deeply indebted to his involvements in Rotary for the contribution it made to his ministry. It afforded him a dimension and a perspective which have been of inestimable value.

When he became a member at the beginning, however, the local club was in dire straits. After a year or so, when it appeared that the club was in danger of losing its charter, Rotary International sent a troubleshooter to Gallup to pick up the charter because the club was not fulfilling the basic requirements and rules. Since the young preacher was not an officer, he was not called into the conference where the problems were discussed.

During the course of the meeting, however, some of the men suggested that if they could get Harry Stagg to become president of the club, he could pull them out of their difficulties and set them on a firmer foundation. The mediator was surprised that they would suggest one so young in years and so new in Rotary, but suggested they call Harry and invite him to the meeting.

Obligingly he went. The arbitrator looked squarely at the Baptist minister and said, "These gentlemen tell me that if you will accept the presidency of this club, they can make it successful and keep their charter. If you will accept this position under these circumstances, I will leave the charter and give the club a chance. Otherwise, I will take the charter back to Chicago tonight."

The previous summer Harry had taken his young family to Alpine, Texas, where the district convention of Rotary was held. They stayed on a dude ranch and enjoyed the experience tremendously. Harry had been asked to attend in the place of the president of the Gallup club, who could not go. He had received such inspiration and information during the sessions that the work of Rotary opened up to him in a challenging way. And so, when confronted with the option of the club's being dissolved if he could not serve, he agreed to do what he could.

Key leadership from the entire county around Gallup was gradually added to the membership. The president threw himself into the work of sustaining the club and was sent as their representative to numerous meetings for directives and help. In 1928 he went to Minneapolis-St. Paul for his first meeting of Rotary International. The very next week he attended his first Baptist World Alliance in Toronto, Canada, a short distance farther on. The magnitude and scope of these two worldwide meetings thrilled the young preacher beyond words because he was surrounded with such dedicated and forceful leadership from around the globe. Before the end of the Alliance, however, Harry's physical strength gave way, and he boarded a train for home. Completely spent in body, he was nevertheless emotionally and spiritually exhilarated by all he had experienced as he returned to his tiny church.

During his first year as president, Dr. Stagg became closely associated with the district governor, Clinton P. Anderson. The warmth of his friendship with Dr. Stagg remained constant through the years until Mr. Anderson's death almost fifty years later. During his years as a member of the Senate in Washington, Mr. Anderson would return to New Mexico for the purpose of using the forum of Rotary to announce major scientific breakthroughs or to give important government releases. And during conversations with Dr. Stagg, there was a mutual exchange of information and encouragement. "Every contact with Senator Anderson," said Dr. Stagg in tribute to his dear friend, "was a call to a higher and more useful purpose in any line in which a man had an opportunity to serve."

After Harry served for a year as president of the Gallup club, the organization was on firm enough footing that the charter was maintained, and another man was elected to head the group. The following year, however, they prevailed on Harry to serve again. In all, he served three full years as president of that local organization.

In 1930, while he was head of the group, he was sent to the world convention. This was the twenty-fifth anniversary of the founding of Rotary and was extremely significant. The special nature of the convocation made it a treasured memory for Mr. Stagg. And during his pastoral days in Gallup, when denominational meetings took him to other parts of the state or nation, he made up meetings in other cities as his schedule allowed. These encounters were made memorable by the instant acceptance in any fraternal club. The friendships made and the public relations enjoyed were valuable in his ministry. In point of fact, the largest single contributor to the first and second buildings of Gallup's First Baptist Church was the Commander of the Knights of Columbus—and a dear Rotary friend.

When the Staggs moved to Albuquerque, Senator Anderson recommended Harry Stagg to membership in that club immediately. Thus, his membership in Rotary has been continuous—his alliance with the Gallup club was intact until his acceptance in the new group. He was to enjoy rapport and every courtesy from the very first. News of his successes with the Gallup Rotary had preceded him, and his deep friendship with the senator gave him a treasured position of regard among his new comrades.

Just before Fidel Castro came to power in Cuba, Harry Stagg directed thirteen leaders from the Southern Baptist Convention on a mission tour into Mexico and Cuba. They visited numerous mission stations in Mexico and twenty in Cuba. He was able to visit Rotary clubs in these nations as well and met the leaders in their own national settings.

When he was on tour of the Holy Land in the winter of 1951-52, he attended a significant meeting in Cairo, Egypt. Egypt was in the throes of one of the major crises of its entire existence. All tourists were stopped at the border; only a few could enter by air, and they were guarded around the clock by Egypt's military forces. The Rotarians gathered in a beautiful hotel looking out over the storied Nile River. Attending were representatives of many nations of the world.

The men were divided into language groups of eight and sat at tables adequate for each party. An interpreter was available at each table to function as required as the program proceeded. It was a time of extreme stress, a period when world leaders had neither solutions nor a forum from which to orate their views. Therefore, on this occasion, the gathering of Rotarians was used as a stage from which to express themselves. Leadership of world industry was present. Diplomats from nations involved were there. Military heads from nations supporting those committed to firm answers were there. And others, concerned by the climate in which they found these nations, were serious listeners. The meeting lasted three hours and was spectacular in world deliberations.

During the years between 1945 and 1949, for the first time in the history of the world, the leaders of a government were brought to trial, charged with perpetrating an aggressive war. Nuremburg, Germany, was the scene of global interest during those awesome days as men such as Goering, Hess, and von Ribbentrop stood before the International Military Tribunal to try to explain their activities. Later industrialists, Hitler's principal officers, doctors accused of cruel medical experiments in concentration camps, and other leaders were brought to Nuremburg for trial. Some were imprisoned; others were acquitted; some were hanged; others committed suicide. In the aftermath of this drama of tragedy and before the ravages of war had been cleared away, Harry Stagg appeared at the Nuremberg Rotary Club and addressed the group of interested listeners. His was a fresh voice of encouragement during a tragic era, one which knew the trauma of war.

He also attended the meeting of the Westminster Rotary Club in London, England; wherever he went in the world, he made friends and gathered information from every stratum of knowledge imaginable. And in his local club, surrounded by the greatest scientific minds and experiments in the world (there are four thousand scientists working in the Albuquerque-Los Alamos laboratories), he was exposed to mind-bending disclosures of developments in nuclear and space sciences as skilled men spoke before Albuquerque's International Club.

When the tenth anniversary of the organization of the United Nations was to be celebrated, seats in the small auditorium were at a premium. For every space available, there were numerous individuals earnestly seeking reservations. The conclave was to be held in San Francisco, in the same locale of the initial organization; it would be a historic occasion. To Harry Stagg's delight and gratitude, Senator Anderson arranged for him to have a pass for that meeting! Leaders from all over the face of the earth appeared and spoke to the gathering, who wore radio headphones for instantaneous translation into their own tongue. The fabulous exhibit provided for their information, and the inspiration and magnitude of the scope of each session gave the minister from New Mexico a perspective of the world which would have otherwise been impossible.

Later Dr. Stagg was invited to attend the Navy War College sponsored by the Eighth Naval District of New Orleans. It was held at Albuquerque's Kirtland Air Force Base. Screened carefully, passing through three lines of security, and swearing an oath of allegiance and secrecy, they were admitted for three days to an area of highly classified information of military data. Astounding facts of past, present, and future were revealed to them. Many of these carefully concealed mysteries have by now passed into the pages of history; others are still in the future.

Another door opened to Dr. Stagg was an invitation to attend the State Department Conference held in the Law School of the University of Denver. Foreign policy makers spoke to leading citizens over the five or six state area. He attended a similar conference at Southern Methodist University in Dallas, Texas, also. The outlook projected in these assemblages further served to broaden the scope of Harry Stagg's knowledge and concern.

In 1953 Dr. Stagg was elected District Governor of Rotary International! He was amazed! The territory covered all of the state of New Mexico, with the exception of Clayton and Raton, and reached into Texas through the El Paso area as far as Alpine and Marfa. When the Baptist Mission Board of the state was apprised of this selection, they immediately voted to grant him adequate time to carry on these additional duties and even offered to help in any expenses not covered by Rotary International! They recognized the value these contacts would have in the Baptist work in the state: wherever their executive secretary traveled, he was first and foremost a Baptist leader. Although Dr. Stagg accepted their gracious gift of time, he judiciously paid for any marginal expenses not covered by Rotary out of his own funds.

As he dealt with the presidents and officers of each club throughout his district, many warm friendships developed and never-to-be forgotten experiences occurred. He conducted the district conference and the district assembly, worked with Rotary International on a personal basis, and spent eight days at the Lake Placid Club for the world assembly, where the bar of the club was padlocked for that period of time. He attended the world convention in 1954 at Seattle, Washington, and the international convention in Chicago, Illinois, the next year. The latter was the memorable fiftieth anniversary of the founding of the club.

The honor of being district governor follows one for the rest of his life. Wherever one goes in the circle of that club—in local, district, or world meetings—special recognition and honor and significant contacts are given. Perhaps Dr. Stagg feels the deepest debt of gratitude to his own club for the honors bestowed on him. In 1974 the Paul Harris Fellow award was given him. This is similar to a degree and is a grant provided by the Rotary Foundation. In practical terms, it is a cash gift of one thousand dollars to the International Scholarship Fund given in honor of a valuable Rotarian. A beautiful certificate was presented to Dr. Stagg, along with a medal to be worn for dress occasions of Rotary and a lapel pin to wear at any time. Out of the 312 membership in Albuquerque's club, ten hold this high honor.

Throughout his fifty-year membership in Rotary, Harry Stagg has made speeches to many clubs throughout the world. One day as he addressed a district meeting in El Paso, Texas, he recounted the story of his guarding the German prisoners of war when he lay injured outside the cave where the men were housed for the night. After the speech was concluded a large man, tall—and German—stood up. He announced that he was a member of the El Paso Rotary Club and that he was president of a certain local business corporation. "And I want to tell you all," he continued, "that I was one of those prisoners in one of those caves that night. I was so impressed by the conduct of these young American soldiers that I realized that they had something in America that we didn't have in Germany. I made up my mind that night that if I could ever make any kind of opportunity I was going to America. And I was able to do it. I have made a successful business and have enjoyed a wonderful relationship with the people in El Paso." Naturally, the entire group was deeply moved by the circumstances of the program as it dramatically unfolded before them.

Not everything that transpired in the club meetings was planned—or serious! One day when Harry went to retrieve his hat, he found that it was missing. In its place was one identical in style and color. Guessing what had happened to his, he promptly put that hat on his head and left. Two days later the man from whom he had bought the hat telephoned him. "Harry," he began, "would you like to trade headgear?" He explained that he had noted the "exchange" when he had seen Harry's name inside the hat and was nonplussed at his error.

When the local group celebrated its fiftieth anniversary, they met at the Officers' Club at Kirtland Air Force Base. There were many distinguished visitors and guests present, including the Archbishop of Santa Fe. The president asked Dr. Stagg if he would meet that gentleman at the door and escort him to his designated place at the head table. As the Catholic Archbishop and the Baptist leader were proceeding toward the proper spot reserved for the former, Dr. Stagg's wit came to the fore. "I never thought," he teased, "that I would ever see the day when a Baptist preacher could put the Archbishop in his place!" Miles apart in theological thought and ecclesiastical position, they nevertheless became warm personal friends.

One day at a weekly luncheon, the president of a bank, with whom Dr. Stagg had dealt many times in seeking funding for New Mexico Baptists, called him aside. "Harry," he said, "could you lend me a dollar and a quarter for lunch?" (It was a *long* time ago!) And Dr. Stagg relates, his eyes twinkling, "I had the joy of my life in making a cash loan to the man to whom I'd looked across the desk many times to make loans for the convention through the years." Evidently no contract was drawn up or signed; no interest was attached or collateral required!

As these kinds of events took place, Harry Stagg stored them in his fertile brain and "used" them in speeches he made before the club, to the delight of all—and perhaps the amused chagrin of others!

When the Gallup club celebrated its fiftieth anniversary, they invited the Staggs back for that significant occasion, and Dr. Stagg addressed the beloved group. They were treated royally and, in appreciation for the work done in years gone by and as a memento of the memorable occasion, were presented a beautiful Navajo rug by the club.

The basic principles of the organization of Rotary are to be found in the Sermon on the Mount. They are also reminded of the mottos "He profits most who serves the best" and "Service above self." These concepts have led them, along with other projects, to establish the international scholarship which involves 150 nations of the world. Students may be interchanged for education in other countries as they receive grants through the Rotary Foundation. And the Four-Way Test emphasized permeates their thoughts, their speech, and their actions. It asks penetratingly, as a caution to precede one's actions or speech: "Is it true; is it fair to all concerned; will it build goodwill and better friendships; and will it be beneficial to all concerned?" To these high ideals and worthwhile projects, Harry Stagg has been grateful to align himself.

The love, high regard, and esteem Dr. Stagg has earned through his association and work with Rotary through fifty years of membership has left, in turn, some deep impressions with him. He believes that some of the greatest opportunities of his whole ministry have come about through his contact with that group. Wherever he traveled he was able to gather information in every line of endeavor to which human beings address themselves. In turn, he was able to use this rich body of knowledge in speeches wherever he found himself. The perspective he received influenced his planning and procedure for Baptist work in his beloved state. New areas of friendship and influence were also opened to him as he moved among fellow Rotarians. All these contacts mattered to him in everything he did.

In his assessment of his valued fraternal club, Harry Stagg says, "Rotary is one of the greatest organizations for the good of mankind around the world, second only to our Christian movement of faith in the Lord Jesus Christ as a personal Savior and the fellowship and regard in the church for which Christ died."

XII. Epilogue

The true measure of a man is not only viewed by his public performance and stance over a long period of time, but also involves his relationships at home, the staff who works with him on a daily basis, and his colleagues who share similar responsibilities. On none of these fronts did a dichotomy of character appear in the study of the life of Harry Perkins Stagg; the personality is wholly integrated and predictable; he is the same man wherever he appears.

A visit with the two daughters is a pleasant, relaxed experience. Marcia busies herself with a complicated piece of needlepoint while Carol works with skeins of thread, preparing them for a large rug her mother plans to make. Huge glass windows from the joining living room and den reveal a lovely backyard as sunlight filtering through the gently swaying trees dapples the whole expanse. They have lived near their parents all their lives and exult in the joy and support this has brought them. They share a wonderful camaraderie—entering each other's lives visibly when there is need or desire for companionship and then retreating into their own busy schedules once more. Carol, married to Dwight Tope (a fellow Rotarian with her father), is the mother of two sons. Rock was born on the twenty-fifth wedding anniversary of his maternal grandparents, and Chris was born three years later. Marcia and Anthony Cantrell are the parents of five busy children—Jim, Steve, Dick, Jack, and Carol.

"Father was often mischievous as a boy," they remark. "One day he decided that in order to stay on good terms with his parents and to eliminate the spankings, he would just stay out of trouble. And he did! He never again required such discipline."

"We remember his story about Halley's Comet. His mother got him up from bed to view that marvel as it streaked across the sky. It was something to see!"

"One of the most difficult things he ever had to do as a boy," Marcia added, "had to do with his little dog. It must have been a little fox terrier or some small breed. But it belonged just to him, and they were always together. However, when a rabid dog got loose in the countryside, he seemed to cover the whole area, picking fights with other dogs and infecting them with the terrible disease. One day Father realized that his little pet had been in a fight and had been bitten. No one in the family had the heart to take care of the situation, so he called to the little dog, and they started toward the field. Father was only ten or twelve at the time, and he carried his gun. When they reached their destination, Father stopped, and while the little dog looked up at him, he pulled the trigger. He then buried him at the edge of the field and put up a little marker. Then he walked back to the house alone. He has never forgotten that day."

Talking between themselves, they recalled their childhood illnesses. "He was always at the forefront of our care, taking his turn with Mother. When he was ill as a young man, he saw what went into taking care of the sick, and simply pitched in and helped when we were ill."

Carol disappeared momentarily, returning with a beautifully woven basket. "When he was ill," she explained, "Father wove two baskets while lying flat on his back in a hospital. The other one belongs to Marcia. They have been in the family fifty years and more!"

He always brought presents from his trips away from home. Carol remembers a beautiful royal blue velvet dress with red and white embroidery all over the bodice. He returned with carved ivory pendants and earrings from Germany and carved earrings from Mexico.

Even today, they agree, they benefit from his presence on shopping trips. "He just seems to know instinctively what is right."

This memory reminds them of identical dresses their mother made for them before a trip to Florida for the Southern Baptist Convention. Without benefit of pattern, she designed two lovely garments and sewed hundreds of buttons on them. They wore them ever so proudly.

When their father returned home from his work, they would run to greet him. A little custom emerged with this greeting. Dr. Stagg would jingle the change in his pocket; if either of them could guess the exact amount, it was theirs! "It was amazing," they smiled, "how often we were able to come up with the right figure."

He was always generous with them; and Carol remembers, as a result of this generosity and of his desire for them to have many varying experiences, her first plane ride.

While they lived in Gallup a trimotored Ford plane was sent out by Transcontinental Air Transport along a certain route. The purpose was to advertise and create interest in flying. The Staggs were invited to try this out; and although none of them had ever flown before, they purchased tickets for the trip. Carol and her aunt, Happy (Dr. Stagg's sister), went on one flight, while her parents followed a few minutes later. They flew out toward Fort Wingate and viewed their world from a completely different perspective. It was a thrilling experience, fulfilling a dream of the veteran soldier when he watched the planes from the trenches in France and thought, "Someday I'll be up there."

In Gallup, they recalled, their father had often gone into the operating rooms either at the invitation of a doctor-friend or through the request of the patient. He would scrub up with the operating room staff, don mask, robe, and gloves, and stand just behind the surgeon on a small stool. He would never speak a word during the surgical process; but when the doctor left the operating area, the entire procedure would be explained to the minister. Knowing of his interest in medicine, the doctors were most helpful and cordial. And many patients felt a little more confident knowing that Mr. Stagg was nearby praying for them.

"Father still maintains his pilot's license," Carol offers. "And he completely maintains the motor home we share together—that in itself is quite a task."

"He loves to fix things, too," Marcia says. "He keeps bits and pieces of equipment and gets quite a thrill from being able to repair anything. Also, no matter what Mother is doing, he helps her until it is completed."

The daughters agree that their parents have always given an extra measure in their work and to people—"what Granny calls 'lagniappe,' " Marcia adds. They feel that God has aided their father every step of the way. "And we always felt lifted up."

Alma believes her husband can do or fix anything. "But," she recalls with amusement, "he created quite a disturbance the day he attempted to repair an old victrola! After doctoring the creaky parts with oil, he turned it on to check it. Oil sprayed on everything!"

Concerning his messages, his wife says that he has "the happy faculty of taking what has gone before and tying it into the present." And she continues, "He is the best Christian I know. He has never spoken one unkind word to me in fifty years!"

Eunice Hoyland first became associated with the Staggs when they all lived in Gallup. Later she worked on the staff at the Baptist building. One day when her pastor was preaching in Gallup, he related the story of one of his closest buddies who had been killed during the war. In the same company, they had gone to France together and had become best friends. When Harry mentioned his name, Eunice almost came out of her chair! The story concerned her cousin! This further bound the budding and fast-growing friendship that was to last for so many years. "He was always available to the staff," she remembers. "He loved them, and it was mutual."

Jeff Rutherford, who was closely associated with Dr. Stagg as pastor and then as Director for Promotion and Stewardship for New Mexico Baptists, says, "He was and is a giant spiritually, a dynamic leader and a brilliant dreamer. It seemed to me he 'shook hands with God.' I have never heard him say 'we can't do it'—but the dreams never exceeded his prayers and work."

Miss Eva Inlow, who served as WMU director for twenty-five years and more, states: "How well I remember the staff riding all night on the trains to and from meetings in the early days! But Mr. Stagg never asked the state workers to do what he wouldn't do himself. Every branch of the work grew and branched out and increased in influence. It was gradual; it was steady; and it was firmly planted."

In a prominent place in the living room of Harry and Alma Stagg is a prized possession. It is a large book, a bound volume of letters of tribute from their multitudes of friends. Given to them at retirement, it is now interlaced with several death notices of dear friends whose letters are included. From every corner of our country and from every stratum of Baptist life, there are tributes. The majority include deep appreciation of Mrs. Stagg and her abiding support of her husband's ministry.

W. R. Buchanan wrote: "Your presence and inspiring message one morning in 1941 brought new confidence to our small and struggling group and a fresh realization to me that God had revealed his leadership and purpose in our coming back to New Mexico."

Dr. Baker James Cauthen stated: "You have been a constant force for sharing Christ with a world in need."

Dr. W. E. Grindstaff said, "You have turned sickness into health, obstacles into stepping-stones, and disaster into triumph. Your leadership is marked by two characteristics: you have gone somewhere, and you have taken others with you. You have not only led the procession of Baptists in New Mexico, but you chose the route. You cast your bread upon the waters and it returned buttered, covered with jam, wrapped in paraffin paper, and marked 'with love.'"

Dr. Herschel Hobbs stated: "I have known you for more years than either one of us would like to admit. Never have I known you when you did not ring true to the cause of Christ."

Dr. Douglas Hudgins wondered: "How can human evaluation

be made of the contribution you have made to the work of the gospel and the activity of Baptists in your state? Only God could keep such a record!"

And Chester Quarles exuded: "I think you ought to be declared an institution and endowed so that you can serve forever!"

A Spanish pastor, Gilbert Ramos, wrote: "It is like having a tooth pulled that we give you up."

Dr. Porter Routh stated: "The name 'Stagg' has been an honored name in Southern Baptist life for many years and will be carved on the hearts of New Mexico Baptists with deep and abiding strokes."

And his successor, Dr. R. Y. Bradford, said: "I think of you as a man's man, as God's servant, as Mr. New Mexico, as Mr. Baptist—you have been a leader of men, an ambassador for Christ, a booster for New Mexico, and a champion of the rights and causes of Baptists. Your ministry will be characterized by the historians for its length, but by those who have known and worked with you by its depth, its wide scope, and the heights to which you have challenged us to aim and serve."

Today as the Staggs enjoy a "quiet retirement," their lives are still given away to churches who ask for their help, to their children and grandchildren, to other relatives of many states, and to their many friends.

Perhaps the most exciting event in the offing is the celebration of their fiftieth wedding anniversary. Friends and relatives from Texas, Mississippi, Louisiana, Arizona, California, Arkansas, Washington, Alabama, Colorado, and New Mexico will come to pay tribute to the couple. Miss Harriet Gatlin has painted beautiful gold and white china pieces to be used for the occasion. A gold bowl used on Dr. Stagg's parents' golden anniversary will be in evidence. Marcia, skilled in intricate cake decorating, is fashioning the tiered wedding cake. And Carol, a prize-winning weaver, has handwoven and tailored the beautiful gold and white dress her mother will wear. Woven from over fourteen thousand yards of silk thread, the overshot pattern required sixty-four treadle changes to make the overall pattern repeat, which includes her parents' names and the dates, 1926-1976, over and over again in the lovely fabric. To the casual observer, however, it appears as gold stripes bordering the white material.

Places for all the family have been reserved for the worship service that day at the First Baptist Church in Albuquerque, church home of the Staggs for nearly forty years. Home and church have been the pivotal points on which their lives have turned.

When Edwin Mechem was governor of New Mexico, he, along with many from his staff, spent the day at Glorieta, greeting travelers en route by train to the Southern Baptist Convention. Dr. Stagg and several from the Baptist staff served as hosts to the group, many of whom were viewing the undeveloped grounds for the first time. Later the governor, now a federal judge, stated: "Baptist work has been a very strong contributing factor to the improvement of individuals, society, and definitely to culture. I think some kind of birth certificate should be conferred on Dr. Stagg because he has adopted our state and moved ahead so well."

Indeed, Harry Stagg not only adopted the state, but was a prime supporter and booster of it throughout his entire life. He believes strongly that much of the westward and northern expansion of Southern Baptist work can find its roots in the organization of the Baptist Convention of New Mexico in 1912. Before this new work began, he feels, a "status quo" spirit had set in, and the desire for reaching into the "hinterlands" was waning. For a time, there was even a question whether the Home Mission Board was needed any longer! The coming into being of a brand-new convention began like a gentle wind to fan the fires of outreach. And when the New Mexico Convention extended an arm to several churches in Arizona and then later did the same for Colorado, the movement began to snowball. The founding of conventions in Arizona (1928), California (1940), Oregon-Washington (1948), and Colorado (1955) followed this ground-swell in natural fashion. The outreach toward the northeastern part of the United States continued the pattern until today there are Southern Baptist churches in every state in the Union, including Alaska and Hawaii, with thirty-three conventions serving them.

All of this reminds us that we are part of a larger scheme. Those who served in the early, difficult, and often discouraging days are reaping even today, Dr. Stagg asserts, the compound interest of their sacrificial service. The decision in 1912 to affiliate with the Southern Baptist Convention, made by a small majority, has made all the difference in the path Baptist work would follow. Each advancement helps to mold and influence other achievements. And as we look with joy toward the future, may we never lose sight of our glorious heritage or forget those who made the foundations strong.

Bibliography

The Baptist New Mexican. Albuquerque: Baptist Press, 1938-1968.

Encyclopedia of Southern Baptists, Volume 2. Nashville: Broadman Press, 1968.

Fergusson, Erna. *New Mexico: A Pageant of Three Peoples.* Albuquerque: University of New Mexico Press, 1964.

Myers, Dr. Lewis A. *History of New Mexico Baptists.* Albuquerque: Baptist Convention of New Mexico, 1965.

The New Mexico Baptist Annual. Albuquerque: Baptist Convention of New Mexico, 1925-1938.

Nuggets of Golden Memories. Collection of letters.

Rutledge, Arthur B. *Home Missions Since 1845.* Atlanta: Home Mission Board's Division of Communication, 1974.

Stagg, W. L., Jr. *Adolphe Stagg: #2 Life and Work.* Albuquerque: Baptist Convention Press, 1954.

World Book Encyclopedia. Chicago: Field Enterprises Educational Corporation, 1968.